THE MISSING BALUSTER

A BALUSTER CLOSES THE GAPS BETWEEN POSTS
PROVIDING SAFETY FEATURES BY ELIMINATING
EXCESS SPACE THROUGH WHICH
A CHILD COULD FALL

The Missing Baluster

PATRICE SAIMAN

Matador
9 Priory Business Park,
Wistow Road, Kibworth Beauchamp,
Leicestershire. LE8 0RX
Tel: 0116 279 2299
Email: books@troubador.co.uk
Web: www.troubador.co.uk/matador
Twitter: @matadorbooks

ISBN 978 1 80046 284 7

British Library Cataloguing in Publication Data.
A catalogue record for this book is available from the British Library.

Printed and bound by CPI Group (UK) Ltd, Croydon, CR0 4YY
Typeset in 10.5pt Aldine by Troubador Publishing Ltd, Leicester, UK

Matador is an imprint of Troubador Publishing Ltd

This memoir is dedicated to Liz, my wife
Nathalie, Sophie, Oliver, our children,
Our grandchildren,
Hattie, Sebbie, Grace, Raphael
And one more to come

With all my love and care

Contents

Prologue

For many years, my childhood was locked away in the dusty past. I did not search for the key. Instead my time and energy were invested mostly in the present, the now. I focused on what I might do in order to improve the future for my family, my staff and my business.

When I had set my heart on accomplishing success and its pleasures, I was not inspired by my childhood which, by the way, was predominantly spent in Paris. In fact, the more I achieved, the further I seemed to move away from my childhood: I left France and came to live in Britain; I tried to give to my children what I had not been given as a child; in terms of career, I was in my early forties when I took the helm of a multi-million-pound business.

As a boy, I had felt that I was invisible. My life lacked stability. As a man, it was almost as if I became visible and, in time, there came the precious stability of family – Liz, and our children, Nathalie, Sophie and Oliver.

I thought that I was distancing myself from my childhood but I was, inadvertently, moving back towards it. Allow me to clarify.

One day – or two, actually – I came close to death. Afterwards, and during a slow recovery, I was encouraged to reassess my life, my journey – to stop and look back. I saw that the path of my childhood certainly had not been an easy one to tread. You shall see this, too.

Yet it is that same path which led me to the success and triumphs of later life. Without one, would I have the other? There I had been, as an adult, escaping my childhood. I did not acknowledge that, at the same time, I was also savouring the fruits of my own misfortune decades earlier. Maybe the point is that in order to fully know an adult, you must first take a long look at his or her childhood.

*

'The unexplained life,' wrote Socrates, 'is not worth living.' My life needed some explaining, and that's around about the time I embarked on a self-set assignment. I wanted to piece together the jigsaw of my existence, beginning with my early years in France of the 1950s and 60s.

One by one, the pieces came together, the picture became clearer than ever. There was the fascinating and poignant story of my mother and father, and also of the Jews in Paris, who had survived the concentration camps. There were the war years before my birth, and the lustful German commandant. There was a murder, and then there was Paris, struggling to rebuild her romantic self after the Nazi Occupation. (As I write, I notice the date. The Germans surrendered Paris to the Allied troops, on this very day seventy-six years ago.) This was an all-consuming tale of conflict and glamour, and driven by profound versions of two human traits that I would know well when I began as a trader: greed and fear.

What for me began as a project with a purpose – a tale that might be enjoyed by my children and grandchildren – gradually became a mission with greater meaning. So much so, that now you are at the beginning of a manuscript. It has been a fresh challenge, putting pen to paper to share the memories of the first part of my life, specifically my childhood, which was by no means a normal one. Much of it was written during the lockdown that took place during the coronavirus pandemic, in the spring and summer months of 2020.

We can be sure of two things: we cannot escape our childhood and uncertainty is a certainty. Therefore we should embrace uncertainty as if it is a gift, like a puzzle to solve, a challenge to surmount. Despite the uncertainties of my life – and the traumas and upheaval – there have been people who helped me to get where I am today. I am grateful to them, and will be for the rest of my life. Helping others, especially the young in their careers, has been a bit of a hobby of mine, and it is incredibly rewarding. Today, at the age of seventy-one, I believe that I know as much as I will ever know about myself and my achievements.

C'est tout. I will leave you to begin this memoir which, I hope, helps to explain how an extraordinary childhood can lead to an extraordinary life. This is not a self-help book. It is a true story of what happened and what followed. However, if it gives the reader fresh ideas, then I'd be delighted. If just one person feels inspired by the story – inspired to search for the key to their past, or to see that the seemingly impossible is achievable – then my mission has been accomplished, and it has all been worthwhile.

Patrice Saiman
*25*th *August, 2020*

One

Champagne and Coffee

So often extraordinary things happen in ordinary moments. Two incidents come to mind. The first occurred one evening, as I drank a glass of champagne. The second happened one morning, as I made a cup of coffee. On both occasions my life could have ended. Ultimately, these two episodes took me on a journey, beginning with recovery and then, I suppose, further on, towards a destination of discovery.

It was September 1996, and Liz and I had been invited for supper at the home of our friends, Martin and Sheila Shaw. At that time Martin was my boss, and we had known each other for a couple of decades. Liz and I arrived at their house in north London, and were looking forward to a jolly, relaxed evening, just the four of us. The aromas of cooking wafted from the kitchen, and Martin popped opened a bottle of champagne, poured and we clinked glasses. The memory is vivid, though I don't seem to remember what we toasted with the champagne. If we raised our glasses to good health, then the toast was worthless. Within a few minutes of the first sip, I felt an astutely chronic pain in my head.

Liz and our hosts could see I was suffering. 'What's the matter, Pat?'

'I don't know,' I said. 'I don't know what's happening.' I stood, and made my way towards a sofa. 'I'll just lie down for a moment... I'll go and rest for five minutes.' So I lay down and suddenly – well, that's when the pain really kicked in. I was in agony. It was as if there was immense pressure growing within my skull. I had this overwhelming sense that only a hole in my head could relieve the pain. In fact, I'd later find out, that pressure was being caused by an aneurysm. I was having a brain haemorrhage. Blood surged between my brain and cranium, causing the intense pressure.

'I'm going to be sick,' I managed to say, and sure enough I started to vomit. Liz phoned Simon, a close family friend who was also our GP.

'I'm coming right away,' he said. Soon Simon was at my side, got the picture, and called for an ambulance. On Simon's instructions, I was rushed to the National Hospital, in Queen Square, Holborn, where the medical team topped me up with painkillers. 'Do you know where you are?' asked a doctor.

'I must be in a brothel in Mayfair.'

The medical team looked at me, quizzical expressions on their faces. 'No,' said Liz. 'He's making a joke. It's his sense of humour.'

Next, I underwent an angiogram procedure. The surgeon asked, 'Do you want to see what's happening?'

'Why not?' And so I watched. The dye was injected. I felt a strange warmth in my body as the dye progressed through my blood vessels. The doctors, who watched on a screen, were unable to locate the point of the bleed. (Liz and I had been told that the angiogram itself brought a risk of causing more bleeding and this could lead to increased – possibly fatal – damage. There was no choice, however.)

First thing in the morning, the surgeon, Mr Powell, came to see me and Liz. 'I have good news,' he announced. 'There's no need for an operation.'

'Oh, that's brilliant.'

'Indeed it is,' he said. 'But you will have to rest.' During the angiogram the doctors were unable to locate the point of the bleed because by then the bleeding had stopped. While this was presented as good news it transpired that it was bad news, as they could not operate and the aneurysm was still there. I asked Mr Powell, 'I have a flying lesson next Saturday. Will I be all right to do it?'

He replied, 'We'll see.' (He was breaking it to me slowly. It would take a whole year before I could fly again, and a further six months before being allowed to fly alone, not to mention eight months before I could drive.)

I spent about a fortnight in the hospital. I slept most of the time, between eighteen and twenty hours a day, and was awoken every few hours by the pain, which was then relieved by painkillers. I sipped orange juice through a straw and, when alone, kept myself busy by counting the diagonals that formed the pattern on the ceiling above me; this was the constant view from my bed as I had to lie on my back and was forbidden from lifting my head.

What went through the minds of Liz and our children, I am not sure I'd ever be able to appreciate or comprehend. I do know that Liz slept most nights on a mattress on the floor in my room, and she would leave in the mornings, going home for a shower and to see the children. I recall the children coming to see me at the hospital, but these are blurred memories (that'll have been the drugs, perhaps). And I recall asking for some paper and a pencil, and as I lay in bed, I began to write down information about my finances, bank accounts and assets, and who best to contact should I slip away. I have continued with these updates ever since, and without the help of drugs. Then it was time to go home, laden with painkillers to keep me going (though some painkillers gave me vertigo so I had to be careful). I could move around a little, and walk with care. Vertigo would come in sudden bursts and, when it did, all I could do was curl up and count to thirty, and try to convince myself that I was actually safe and lying in bed. Once the feeling had subsided, I'd stay still just in case movement set it off again.

*

This takes me to the second occurrence: the extraordinary event in the midst of ordinary when it seemed my time was up.

I'd been out of hospital for a couple of months, and was back at home and recovering. One morning, around seven, I came downstairs with the intention of making myself some coffee. I filled and switched on the kettle. Then I shuffled to the other side of the kitchen, to take a seat at the table as the kettle boiled. The bubble of water, the steam, the click of the kettle – all very ordinary. I stood up and began to make my way back to the kettle and then – bang! It was as if I'd been struck really hard on the back of the head. I fell to the floor.

Liz must have heard the thud, and it seemed that instantly she was there at my side, followed by our children, Nathalie, who at the time was nineteen years old, Sophie, seventeen, and eleven-year-old Oliver. For a moment I wondered if I had fallen asleep. The next thing I knew, the ambulance had arrived. The pain was unbearable, and when I swore at the paramedics Liz apologised on my behalf. She came with me in the ambulance, and Nathalie followed in her car with Sophie and Oliver. I have never dared ask what they were thinking at that moment because I wouldn't want to jog that particular memory (maybe one day).

Next, I was in the Royal Free Hospital. Once again, Simon was called. He made arrangements for me to be returned to the National in Queen Square, and come evening that is where I found myself, in the Nuffield private ward. A variety of painkillers saw me through, along with sleep, and that day is a fuzzy memory. As I had come from another hospital, I was put in an isolation unit, tests were conducted, and the decision was made to give me another angiogram. I signed the consent form – was there a choice? – and the doctors located the bleed. Mr Powell recommended a new consultant, Neil Kitchen, a brain surgeon and specialist in aneurysms that happen in the frontal lobe. And so it was Mr Kitchen who said, 'We have to operate.'

That was quite a tough time, much more for Liz than for me. She was not joking when she asked Mr Kitchen to go to bed early so that he could get a proper night's sleep before the operation. 'And don't have anything to drink.'

I had my own chat with Mr Kitchen, just him and me. I said, 'OK, so there are three possibilities. First, that I recover. That would be excellent. The next possibility is that I die. Well, that's what it is. And the third possibility is that I lose the ability needed to look after myself. That's not on. That's not acceptable.'

'You are in very good hands,' he said.

'I know I am in very good hands.' Clearly, I was, because I am here to relay our little chat.

Liz spent another night in my room, mattress on the floor, and first thing the following morning I was taken to the operating theatre. Before I was wheeled in, Liz kissed me. Although I was on a variety of mind-numbing drugs, I wondered whether she thought she was kissing me goodbye. And then… my skull was opened and the aneurysm was clipped.

A couple of days after the operation, I was lying in bed with bandages around my head, when Mr Kitchen, accompanied by a few of his students, came to discuss my case. His tie was quite colourful, and I said, 'Did you have curry last night?' Which I thought was funny but, again, Liz apologised for my comment. 'It's Pat's sense of humour.' Whether this was actually appreciated by Mr Kitchen or his students remains questionable, but was probably excused by the infamous drugs.

I followed this gaffe a couple of days later when I heard a patient in a neighbouring room shouting swear words at the nurses. There happened to be a nurse in my room, and I said to her, 'Maybe you should pull his plug.'

She replied, 'You didn't hear yourself after your operation.' I found out that when you have an operation on the brain, your inhibitions (I do have some) vanish. So there we are, that's my excuse.

Nathalie would come after work and play chess with me, and we'd share my dinner which was served by a lovely Irish guy. When he was asked for a specific food, he'd say, 'Oh, want, want, want… that's all I hear,' and then he'd disappear to the kitchen and return, with a smile, bringing whatever had been ordered. I spent a lot of time sleeping. I managed to keep my mobile phone under my pillow, and my Moroccan buyers, who'd heard that I'd been taken ill, texted to say that they kept a tonnage for us, although we had not participated in a tender. So, while in bed, I managed to book an order without even lifting a finger. That never happened again, unfortunately, but it demonstrated the quality of the relationship we had built, and I was touched.

Some weeks after leaving hospital, I returned for a consultation with Mr Kitchen. He looked at me, paused for a moment, and then said, 'Is your eyebrow working well?'

I said, 'Erm, yes.'

'It's just that I was a bit concerned about it. I thought I may have damaged a nerve.'

'In terms of my problems,' I said, 'the prospect of not being able to move my eyebrow is not really a consideration. If my eyebrow stops working, I think I can deal with it.'

When I was discharged from hospital it was on certain conditions. These were the same conditions I had heard after the first brain haemorrhage. Namely that I could not drive for twelve months. I was also told not to travel and, in fact, not to leave London for that same period of time. Also, I was instructed to be around people, to avoid being alone, just in case I required help.

I became quite friendly with Mr Kitchen, the surgeon. Neil and I share a passion for football. He is an Arsenal supporter, but I know that Manchester United are the greatest. One day, some years after my brain haemorrhages, these two teams were playing at Old Trafford. I invited Neil to watch them with me. As a pilot, I would fly the two of us to Manchester. He arrived, and I greeted him with the words, 'Now your life is in my hands.'

I remember he said, 'I always carry my little knife, just in case.' The flight went well, and his stained tie was never mentioned again.

I reminded him of our conversation after the first brain haemorrhage, when my situation had been described as "good news". Neil explained this to me. He said something like, 'It was good news that the blood had coagulated at that point. And that's why we told you at the time not to leave London, and to be around others, and not to travel. The most likely scenario of a bleed in the brain is if the aneurysm is not clipped then it will bleed again. But what are we going to tell you, Pat? That you are a time bomb? That at any time it could happen again? We had to wait.'

He told me that many people go through life with an aneurysm, a little bubble lurking in their blood system. 'Most people who have an aneurysm will live all their lives without it ever bursting… and then it's something else that causes their death. Well, we can't say to everybody that we'd like to do an MRI scan to see if there's an aneurysm, because we can't see it until it bursts. It's a failure somewhere. And Pat, when you came back the second time, the aneurysm was there. We then opened up, clipped it and that was that.'

He added, 'We told you not to leave home and not to drive, and to be with your family. Which was the truth. That was all you needed to know.' In other words, I was informed on a need-to-know basis.

By the way, a couple of years after my operation, I would return to the hospital. I was in good health and did not need to go back, but I wanted to. I wanted to walk through the emergency doors that lead to the ward. I arrived and explained to the matron that I had been a patient. 'Do you mind if I sit by the entrance?' She agreed. I sat there for maybe a couple of hours. That was where I could have died.

'Would you like a cup of tea?' asked the matron. Shortly afterwards I left, happy to be still alive.

*

Anyway, there I was, on the road to recovery. For the first few months the slightest exertion of energy left me feeling exhausted. By month six, I got fed up not driving so broke the doctor's rule of a year-long ban from the roads. Liz had slipped out and I decided to drive my car to a supermarket in Golders Green, only a mile from home. For the first time in six months I was alone, and the mere act of shopping for a bottle of milk made me feel like a free man.

Yes, physically I was making progress. Mentally, however, I was extremely flat. So flat that there was nothing which really excited me in any way. There was nothing which depressed me in any way, but there was nothing to bring excitement. It was, as I say, simply that flat feeling. I was no longer what I was. Liz could tell me we were going somewhere, and that was fine. And she could say we were going nowhere, which was also fine.

Liz saw how desperate I had become and suggested to her long-term psychoanalyst that she would give up her analysis if she would agree to see me. That was quite a display of love. But it did not work out like that. Instead, Liz's analyst recommended a lady who was described as "fantastic". I said, 'Yes, I'll see her. No question.'

Anne-Marie Sandler was fantastic, there's no question about it. She was also Swiss-born, Jewish and enormously distinguished. Her husband had been a disciple of Sigmund Freud, and Anne-Marie had worked closely with Anna Freud, daughter of Sigmund, and had been a regular visitor to the Freuds' family home in Hampstead (20, Maresfield Gardens; today it is The Freud Museum).

When I met Anne-Marie she was seventy-five years old. I went to her home, a house in Circus Road, St John's Wood, where she also had her practice. She greeted me and we climbed the stairs to a little room, a comfy snug. In this peaceful environment, my psychotherapy began. 'We'll do three sessions,' said Anne-Marie, 'and then I'll see who I can recommend to you.' To the two of us, this was to be just a short spell of consultations – merely a few sessions, no more. She would assess me, see if I could benefit from therapy, and then recommend another therapist, the right person.

As it transpired, there would never be another therapist. When I say that I was not depressed, I might perhaps amend that. I was, in fact, depressed. I had realised I could not function. Liz had softly steered me towards therapy, but had also said, 'You do need to see somebody.'

By the end of the third or the fourth session there was no doubt in Anne-Marie's mind, and definitely none in my mind, that she was the right person. Fifteen years later I asked her how long it would take for her to assess me, and she replied, with her kind smile, 'I am quite slow.'

In those early sessions we spoke in French and then, as we progressed, we conversed in English. There were a lot of tissues that I got through, and plenty of periods of silence, but it was perhaps the most rewarding (and the hardest) experience I had encountered. What a journey and "she who must be obeyed" had saved my life. Anne-Marie would listen as I went back to my childhood in France... back to the chaos, the drama, the deaths, back to the creation of my inspiration, my hero, my God.

With Anne-Marie I could be myself, and could talk to her about absolutely anything. Our sessions continued, as I say, for the next fifteen years. She listened, she cared, she paused, she advised me on anything. I felt secure with her. She adapted her schedules to suit my travelling, and was available on the phone when I needed her.

At the age of ninety she "retired" and, as far as our sessions were concerned, that was it. The story, it seemed, came to an end, the curtain came down.

She had helped me out of a hole. She had helped me to make some sense of my early years. So often extraordinary things happen in ordinary moments and, in one respect, there was nothing unusual about my relationship with Anne-Marie. It was routine, run-of-the-mill therapist-patient stuff. However, as I sat with Anne-Marie, re-tracing my life and examining the relationship with my mother, an extraordinary thing happened. I did have a mother, but Anne-Marie became the mother I *felt* that I never had.

Two

Marcelle and the Apple

A mong the German troops stationed in Paris during the Occupation, there was a certain commandant whose name was Salffner. Since that day in June 1940, when the tanks of the Panzer division thundered down the Avenue des Champs-Elysées, Parisians had been under the watchful eye of the officers who had taken control of their city, and Salffner had a particularly watchful eye.

The world was suffering and at war, but this soldier lived comfortably in an apartment in Villa Bagatelle, a grand house on rue Racine in the sixth arrondissement. For him, the hardships of conflict were softened not only by having his own private accommodation in a pretty street, but also by a butler who indulged the commandant, tending to his wishes and needs.

One day the commandant visited Deauville, the picturesque seaside town on the north coast, some 200 kilometres from the capital. Once it had been a fashionable spot for tourists, but since the outbreak of war it was occupied by the German air force. The Luftwaffe considered this northern part of France a convenient place for airfields, the British shores being a short flight away.

Strolling through the streets of Deauville, seagulls screaming above him, Salffner came to the marketplace and then he stopped to observe a young woman. Perhaps he paused because he could see what she was doing. Or maybe it was her beauty that stopped him in his tracks – her striking, dark brown eyes, and brown curly hair. Marcelle's hair was always immaculate. Yet Salffner did see the young woman commit a crime. Hardly the most serious crime these days – she stole an apple from a stall. With the food shortages of war, however, the theft of food was no light matter.

Did the stallholder see what happened? Again, I don't know. But Salffner saw the theft, and he approached the young woman and tapped her shoulder, gently. She turned and, for a moment, was alarmed. The officer – handsome in his gleaming uniform – was the Enemy, standing in front of her. She was frightened to be caught out, panicky. There was no need for her to be concerned. The German officer took pity on her. 'What is your name?'

'Marcelle.'

Marcelle-Andrée Boissière was about twenty years old, and I can tell you a little about her background. She was born in Deauville on 9th July 1922, and was the eldest daughter of a working-class Catholic couple. Her father, Jean, hailed from Brittany and her mother was Aline. As well as Marcelle and her two sisters, Thérèse and Michele, the three eldest children in the Boissière family were sons: Jean, Bernard and André. A fourth son had died at birth. The Boissières lived at 115 rue de Verdun, not far from the River Touques.

Marcelle's role in the family was that of carer to her younger sisters. That, and to keep the house clean. Perhaps, too, it was as a child that she learnt to knit, and, with her mother in the kitchen, that she learnt to cook skilfully. Marcelle had a musical ear and sang well, with a voice that was quite high, or alto. Those songs from her childhood, such as "Roses de Picardie", would remain some of her favourites. She could play the violin and dreamt that one day she would learn to play the piano, though the dream was never realised.

While her mother was passive, Monsieur Boissière was severe. He would make her polish the plates, and once she'd finished tidying up, he would carry out inspections. If he found a speck of dust or dirt, grime or grease, he'd make her do it all over again. He was severe enough, maybe, for Marcelle to yearn to escape, to have her independence. Which she accomplished at the age of seventeen – or was it even younger? – when, around the outbreak of the war, she left home and trained to be a hairdresser.

Marcelle was about nineteen years old when she met the man who would become her first husband. Jean-André-Maurice Philippon was born on 9th April, 1919 in Issoudun, an ancient town in the department of Indre and Vierzon, in the Centre-Val de Loire region. When he met Marcelle, Jean was living in Flers, a two-hour drive from Deauville. And it was in Flers, and in the latter months of 1942, that Marcelle and Jean's child was conceived. Marcelle and Jean didn't live together for long.

*

Marcelle was pregnant when the theft of an apple led her to meet the German commandant at that market stall in Deauville. Salffner had a few things in his favour. In his heart he was neither a Nazi nor SS, and he was especially handsome. At that meeting in Deauville, he invited Marcelle and a friend of hers to come to Paris, where they could visit him at the Villa Bagatelle. They went. Marcelle stayed. The soldier and his lover were united by an apple, that ancient symbol of love and fertility. Marcelle, the pregnant trainee hairdresser who was turning twenty, moved in to the officer's lavish apartment, with butler in attendance. The commandant spent his days at the senate of the Luxembourg Palace, while Marcelle busied herself, perhaps shopping for food and then cooking for her officer, and awaiting the arrival of her child.

Marcelle's daughter was born in Paris on 4th June, 1943. Salffner was there at the birth, and Jean, of course, was not. She was born in a clinic in rue Lauriston, brought into the world by the clinic's midwife, Madame Gauthier. Marcelle would later tell her daughter, 'Beside the clinic there was a building which was the Gestapo headquarters. The screams of women in labour were drowned out by the horrific screams of people who were being interrogated next door…'

The commandant presented Marcelle with the gift of a pretty cradle, and said, 'She is not mine. But I will look after her, and you… and she must wear the most beautiful dresses.'

The child was named Norma. This name is not French, of course, and it was apparently the commandant who suggested it. Perhaps he was inspired by one of the great Hollywood actresses of the time, Norma Shearer. The actress – the first to be nominated five times for an Academy Award – liked to play the roles of sexually-liberated women. She was 'the first American actress to make it chic and acceptable to be single and not a virgin on screen'. The star was largely responsible for the popularity of the name: thousands of parents named their new-born daughters Norma. One of Norma Shearer's last movies, *Escape*, was released in 1942. In it, she played a single woman, a widow, who is having an affair with a German officer.

At the town hall, Norma was judged not an appropriate French name, however. For the official records, therefore, she was Jocelyne Marianne Anne Marie. In the same records, and in the entry for the father's name, the word "unknown" was written. This meant that Norma took her mother's surname, rather than Jean's. And in the process, Marcelle could deliver a typically characteristic rebuff to Jean.

14

The end of the war brought about the end of the relationship between the young French woman and her German lover. In August 1944 the German army left Paris, retreating back to Germany. Salffner gave Marcelle some money, and then he was gone. In the years to come, when others would speak of the horrors of the Occupation, Marcelle could silence a room when she'd say, 'You know, the war was really not so bad, after all.'

Shortly after the Germans left Paris, the troops of the Second French Armoured Division, led by General Philippe Leclerc – mostly known by his nom de guerre, Leclerc – made its way into Paris. They were soon followed by Allied troops, who arrived in force, and, amid the euphoria, the city was liberated.

Crowds of Parisians who had shuddered as the tanks thundered down the Champs-Elysées four years ago, were now waving, singing, crying tears of happiness because of what they had gained, and tears of grief because of what they had lost during the Occupation. Then, from the Hôtel de Ville, de Gaulle made a rousing speech: 'This duty of war – all the men who are here and all those who hear us in France – know that it demands national unity. We, who have lived the greatest hours of our history, we have nothing else to wish than to show ourselves, up to the end, worthy of France. Long live France!'

After the celebrations, it was time for vengeance. In the weeks that followed, and in the liberated cities and towns across the country, French women who had "collaborated" with the Nazis were gathered up and underwent ritual humiliation: in front of cheering mobs, the women's heads were shaved, and then they were paraded through the streets in the backs of trucks, jeered and shouted at by the masses. To some they were "prostitutes". To others they were "les poules à Boches", the Germans' hens. Marcelle was spared this public ridicule. One day, before she could be dragged into a local square, she took the clippers and shaved her head. Her hair was gone, and the job was done. The most memorable haircut she ever gave was to herself, on that day.

Next, she returned to Jean, the pharmacist. This time, with their daughter as a catalyst, they tried again, another stab at their relationship. They were married, and Norma was recognised as Jean's child. The child's surname was changed officially from Boissière to Philippon. But it was a marriage which was not destined to last. That second stab at romance had proved fatal to the relationship. Marcelle would later laugh as she recalled, 'One day Jean told me that he was going to buy some milk. He never returned.'

Jean moved to Cambodia and in Phnom Penh he continued to work as a pharmacist, and it would be years before he saw his daughter again.

As for Norma, she did not live with her mother, Marcelle. Instead, the little girl was sent to live with Marcelle's parents in Deauville. At her maternal grandparents' home, Norma was also cared for by her young aunt Michele, who was a student. Michele taught Norma to knit, and at bedtime she would read to her, books such as *Gulliver's Travels*. Norma did not feel alone in her new home. On the contrary, she may have been without her mother and father, but she was content, for now at least.

Three

Raoul and the Topaz

As Salomon Raoul Saiman made his way through the post-war streets of Paris on his way to the meeting, he may have allowed himself a moment to reflect on his life, his origins.

Born into a Jewish family in Algiers on 25th January, 1900, he was a bright child, and went on to study law. Then he had come to Paris, where he began work for his Uncle Léonce, his father's younger brother, at his legal practice in Paris. From there, Raoul (he did not use his first name, Salomon) was on his way to becoming a success, but one day he was almost stopped by a bullet.

He was thirty years old, and it was the summer of 1930, when he cheated death in a bizarre incident. Abraham Krauss was an Argentinian citizen and clearly psychotic, as we shall see. He was also enraged about an inheritance issue that had been handled by Léonce Saiman.

Krauss believed that he was the sole beneficiary of his late brother's estate, and he became enraged when the will was contested. He was looking for revenge, which, at eleven o'clock on the morning of 30th July, took him to Monsieur Saiman's office, on the second floor of 2, rue Hippolyte Lebas, in the 9th arrondissement. Krauss was accompanied by his friend, Aseo Nissim.

There, the two men were greeted by Raoul. At first, there was no sign of trouble. Krauss and Raoul shook hands, but as they did so, the Argentinian tightened his grip and brought Raoul towards him. Suddenly, with his other hand, he pulled a revolver from his pocket, and fired twice. Miraculously, Raoul avoided being hit by either bullet, even though they were fired at such close range. The young lawyer freed himself from the grip, and ran into another office, where he phoned for the police.

Nissim, meanwhile, screamed at his friend, 'You're crazy.' He grappled Krauss to the ground, and during the scuffle two more shots were fired. Nissim was killed. The police arrived, and Krauss was arrested. The murder made a dramatic story on the front page of the following day's edition of *Le Petit Parisien*. Maybe after that episode, Raoul paused to reflect on destiny and death. As the Russians say, 'If your destiny is to be hanged, you shall never drown.'

*

Diligent and pragmatic, Raoul was also clever and wise, and his quick wit had helped him in his career and in his personal life – he was highly likeable, known for his charm and good humour. Raoul had established an excellent reputation as a lawyer and as a soldier during the war. He was what they call a survivor.

Here he was, at the age of forty-seven, a war hero. As World War II had drawn to an end two years earlier, he had been decorated with honours and medals. These included the Medaille des Evades, awarded to prisoners of war who had managed to escape internment. He had Le Croix de Guerre 1939–1945, awarded for acts of heroism. He had the Cross of the Second Armoured

Division, and the Cross of The Liberation of Paris. He was one of those who helped to push the Nazis, including Commandant Salffner, into retreat. In the fight against the Germans, Saiman had proved himself to be a brave and distinguished Frenchman.

So much so, that Raoul had also been appointed Chevalier de la Légion d'Honneur, the highest decoration that can be awarded to any Frenchman. Among his correspondence, meanwhile, there was a letter of praise from General Leclerc, who had led the Second Armoured Division in the Liberation of Paris. Behind Raoul's demeanour of confidence and assuredness, however, there were the memories of loss and heartache, the inevitable scars of war.

But let's go back two decades, to Paris in 1927, the year that Raoul's girlfriend, Henriette Rosenberg, gave birth to the couple's daughter, Danièle-Nicole. She would be their first and only child. The three of them lived in a large and comfortable apartment in Pigalle, at 2, Square La Bruyère. Raoul and Henriette were married on 3rd January, 1931, when Danièle was three years old.

In later years, Danièle would look back on her early childhood in those pre-war years, and describe it as an "idyllic" period. The family home, the whole atmosphere of the place, was vastly improved by the presence of Renée and Joseph Sagot, a couple who were on Raoul's payroll. Renée was the housekeeper, while her husband, Joseph, was the Saimans' chauffeur. They were a popular, cheerful couple, and they brought a certain harmony to the Saiman household.

The Saimans lived on the fourth floor, in luxury, and the Sagots lived on the sixth floor of the same building. In the residential buildings of Paris, the highest floor is usually the servants' accommodation, accessed via a service staircase.

I hesitate before describing the Sagots' home as an "apartment". It was more like servants' quarters, with a kitchenette, kitchen table, and a couple of chairs, so that it was also a dining room and living room. The couple's trusty radio was usually playing as Renée cooked meals to carry downstairs for the Saimans, or prepared food for herself and her husband. There was a curtain which hung across the middle of the kitchen, on the other side of which there was a small bedroom. Elsewhere on the sixth floor there was a bathroom. That was it, the Sagots' home – not much, and with a kitchen and bedroom separated by a curtain, but the place was cosy and warm, reflecting very much the spirit of the two people who lived there.

Renée and Joseph were far more than committed employees. They were considered part of the Saiman family, and young Danièle regarded them as her grandparents.

Then came the outbreak of war and subsequently the German invasion of France. Raoul, at about the age of forty, joined the French army, and he was gone, fighting an unwinnable war against the German troops as they advanced through France. Had Henriette and Danièle stayed in Paris, their future would have been grim, though they might not have known just how grim. They would have been rounded up like the other Jews, and sent on a cattle train to a concentration camp, eventually to be gassed.

Instead mother and twelve-year-old daughter escaped the metropolis and the Enemy, and they fled with their loyal servants, Renée and Joseph. (As the Saimans' beautiful apartment was the property of Jews, it was destined to be confiscated by the Nazis.)

Henriette, Danièle, Renée and Joseph headed north, and settled in the Sagots' home town of Berck-sur-Mer, which sits on the shores of the English Channel and is about fifteen kilometres from Le Touquet. There, they pretended to be a family: Joseph and Renée told others that they were the parents of Henriette, and the grandparents of Danièle. It was a charade, a lie, an essential wartime invention. To complete this non-Jewish story, Danièle was baptised a Catholic. Appropriately enough for this secret "family" who were relying on the safety of silence, their home in Berck was at 2, rue du Silence, and the house still stands today.

As the weeks progressed, Henriette became increasingly anxious, fearing that she would be caught. She was Jewish, she looked Jewish and she was now living in a small town. There would be chit-chat and gossip. Surely it was just a question of time, she reckoned, before she would be denounced, and the Gestapo would come to take away her and her daughter.

So Henriette came up with a plan. She would leave behind Danièle with Renée and Joseph, and make her way to the southwest of France, which at that point was a free zone, not occupied by the Nazis. Here, she would be safe. Perhaps she felt that Danièle would be safest with the Sagots.

Henriette needed someone to help her with the escape. *Passeurs* were the heroic French smugglers of the war. They smuggled weapons into the country, and got them to the Resistance fighters, and they smuggled people – Jews – to a place of safety, either by helping them to leave France, or by taking them to the free zone. Sadly, there were often crooks who claimed to be *passeurs*. They would promise to help with the escape but then, during the journey to safety, they would kill the Jews before stealing their money and possessions.

One night, Henriette left with a *passeur*, that much is known. Danièle would never forget the night when, after supper, she kissed her mother goodbye. Six decades later, and over a lunch in London, Danièle shared her recollections of that last supper. 'After eating with Renée and Joseph, my mother took me upstairs and read me a story. She said, "I have to go out for a while. But I'll be back…" I fell asleep.'

In the morning, Renée and Joseph were there, but Henriette had gone. Henriette was assumed dead, though her body was never found. Danièle remained hopeful, for some time at least. She believed that her mother had simply disappeared and was suffering from amnesia. 'I know she will return,' she would tell herself.

*

Danièle would have to wait a few years to be reunited with her father, but at least they had both survived. While Danièle's war was spent anxiously awaiting her mother's return, Raoul's war was packed with adventure, travel and encounters with the highest-ranking commanders of Free France.

He had joined the army in 1939, and then, in the weeks following the Fall of France in May 1940, he was one of the many French troops who surrendered and was placed under arrest and held in a prisoner of war camp. When he was later awarded the Medaille des Evades, the citation read:

'Good non-commissioned officer of an anti-tank unit taken prisoner during the Campaign of France, near Chateaubriand on 18th June, 1940. Locked up in the prison camp in Morencey, he managed to escape on 27th October, 1940, reached the unoccupied zone and embarked for Mexico, to make himself available to the Forces Françaises Combattantes (French Fighting Forces).'

Raoul had made several escape attempts before this successful one, which was probably about the time that his wife, Henriette, was plotting or making her own escape from the north of France to the Free Zone. In the case of his escape, Raoul was assisted by his mistress. She was Jewish and her family lived in Mexico, and she also happened to know a German officer. She bribed the officer who, in turn, enabled Raoul's escape from the prison camp.

Raoul now made his own journey to the Free Zone, and from there he took the first boat to Brazil. He was not penniless because his mistress had arranged for him to be given money, and quite a bit of it. She went to Mexico to join her family, and she waited for Raoul to join her.

Now, at the time, French banknotes were large and it was not safe to travel with a weighty number of francs. And it just so happened that the world's finest and most valuable topaz – the reddish-orange "imperial topaz" – is found in the mines of Ouro Preto, the colonial town in the south-eastern Brazilian state of

Minas Gerais. Well, Raoul was in Brazil and he was smart and innovative. He bought a precious topaz stone, thereby diminishing his hefty pile of cash. He could always sell the gem if he needed money urgently. Then he travelled north to Mexico, to join his mistress, the thoughtful, wealthy and considerably well-connected woman who had enabled his escape. She wanted to marry Raoul, but he was reluctant.

He was, after all, married to Henriette. How long he stayed in Mexico is unclear, but it is certain that he did not want his war to end. He probably could have ducked out of combat in Mexico, had he chosen to. But he chose not to. Raoul's war was far from finished.

He made his way to London, where General de Gaulle was living in exile. Raoul's journey took him first by ship to the United States. Then in New York he boarded a small steam ship, *Egyptian Prince*, and crossed the Atlantic, stopping first in Belfast, before arriving in Cardiff on 3ʳᵈ October, 1942. On the embarkation papers, his proposed address in the United Kingdom was: 'c/o Free French Forces. 4 Carlton Gdns, London.' The documents also show that, strangely, he was the only passenger on board the *Egyptian Prince*.

In London, Raoul met with General de Gaulle, who was heading the French free forces and who was living in Golders Green at the time. 'You come from Algiers,' said the general.

'I was born there.'

'I want you to go there. Go to Algiers and meet General Leclerc. He is over there right now.' Raoul left and, with a letter of introduction from de Gaulle, he now trekked off to Algeria's capital. Once there, he went to the Free French Army headquarters, which today is where you will find the French Embassy. A man, minus his shirt, was shaving beneath the shade of a tree. He saw Raoul and asked, 'What do you want?'

'I want to see General Leclerc.'

'You are looking at him,' replied the man with the foam on his face. General Philippe Leclerc, as commander of the Second Armoured Division, would later lead the Liberation of Paris.

Apart from being united with Leclerc, Raoul was reunited with the family he had left many years earlier. His father, Maurice, was the older brother of Raoul's former employer, Uncle Léonce. Maurice was thirty years old when he married nineteen-year-old Clotilde in 1900. Raoul was born in the same year, and was to be adored as the family's only son. Next, there were his sisters Esther, Flavie, Rachel and Juliette, who was fourteen years younger than Raoul. They had not heard from Raoul since the outbreak of war – there was no foreign postal service in operation – and had become convinced that he had been killed.

Raoul's adventures in Algiers included taking fellow soldiers on a visit to one of the city's brothels, where prostitutes greeted them with a rendition of La Marseillaise. Among the soldiers was Louis Jacquinot, who would become a minister under de Gaulle's first government.

Jacquinot was born in Lorraine and, at the age of sixteen, had gone off to fight at the outbreak of World War I. He had been appointed to the post of Interior Minister but in June 1940, around the time Raoul was being interned in the prisoner of war camp, Jacquinot resigned to go off and fight on the front. When he was wounded, he joined the French resistance group Alliance, and then went to London, to play a commanding role in Free France. Jacquinot was gay, which was controversial at the time. He kept his sexuality a secret but Raoul told the madam of his preference. Much later on after the war, when Louis Jacquinot was a minister under the first government under general de Gaulle and continued his ministerial duties under various governments, my mother would accompany Jacquinot to government receptions so that the rumours about his sexuality would be somewhat uncertain.

Raoul returned to France, landing with the troops in Toulon, as the Allied forces began their push from the south before D-Day. Raoul was there, with Leclerc, for the Liberation of Paris. Among his possessions, there was a letter from Leclerc, dated 13th October 1944, and beginning 'Mon Cher Saiman'. The general wanted '... to express to you all my satisfaction for the zeal and dedication that you have always shown in the accomplishment of your duties...'

He was Jewish, but his war record and his acquaintance with de Gaulle and Leclerc enabled him to return to his flat without any resistance. Soon he restarted his legal practice but he stayed close to the new government. Although he was a well-decorated soldier, he was neither arrogant nor boastful. He preferred to be in the wings rather than centre stage. 'Much better and safer to pull the strings,' he would say, 'and let others take the credit.'

*

Then came the end of the war, and the world was reunited. Raoul and Danièle were once again together, father and daughter, in Paris. She was aged seventeen, a young woman, and motherless. He was forty-five years old, a widower. The loyal Renée and Joseph returned to their quarters on the sixth floor. Raoul reacquired his flat, which had been acquisitioned by the Nazis during the war.

They shared the apartment, but the harmony of the pre-war years was lacking. Danièle, no longer the child that her father had known, believed that she would look after Raoul. She wanted to cook for him and keep their home tidy. She wanted it to be the two of them, united by what they had been through.

However, Raoul had other plans for achieving harmony. Often, he received young women at his flat, women who were perhaps in their early twenties, not much older than Danièle. She was still grieving the loss of her mother, and yet here was her father, frequently *entertaining* – to use the word of that period – ladies who were half his age. Raoul, rather than be cared for by his seventeen-year-old daughter, was happiest when seeing his girlfriends. His favourite was called Marianne Le Berre, who seemed to visit more frequently than the others.

It was all too much for Danièle – and there was more to come. Her father, having survived the war, wanted to live a little. He suggested that he rent an apartment for Danièle. It was just half a mile or so from his own one in Square La Bruyère. Danièle agreed to his suggestion, and she moved out.

Raoul had also resumed his career as a barrister, *un avocat à la Cour*. And it was around this time that Albert Goldenberg came into his life. Albert met Raoul and it was almost as if instantly they were great friends. Raoul was thirteen years Albert's senior, but the age gap made no difference. They really clicked. Albert was a successful restaurateur, on his way to earning the reputation as "the doyen of Jewish restaurateurs in Paris". Before the war, he had run a delicatessen in Montmartre. Following the war, he had opened a delicatessen in rue des Rosiers, in the historic Jewish quarter of Paris. His new friend, Raoul, had put money into the venture.

Four

The Goldenberg Avengers

The story of Albert Goldenberg and his family is a harrowing, familiar tale of the Nazi persecution of the Jewish people. Albert's parents were Turkish, and had moved to France after World War I, and settled in Paris. They had ten children, among them Albert and his brothers Simon and Jo. Shortly after the German Occupation of Paris, one of the siblings – a seventeen-year-old – befriended a Chilian man. His name was Roi (as in French for king) and he was fifty years old, or so. Jews were being rounded up by the Nazis, and Roi offered to help the Goldenberg family avoid being arrested. He was sinister and devious and he sensed an opportunity to make money, but for the Goldenbergs, Roi's promise of help was deeply reassuring. This came down to trust, and it seems that they trusted him. There he was, a saviour, although in return for protection and silence he requested constant funding from the Goldenbergs.

What they did not know was that Roi had an office in rue Lauriston, in the same building as the Gestapo headquarters.

In 1942 there was a mass roundup of Jews in Paris that took

place over two days in the middle of summer – 16th and 17th July. It would come to be known as 'the Vel' d'Hiv Round Up'. Of the 13,152 Jews who were arrested over those two days, about 5,000 of them were sent to the camp at Drancy, an hour's train journey from the capital. Drancy was an assembly point, where Jews were held before being despatched to concentration camps such as Auschwitz. The Nazis were assisted by French police and authorities, and many of those arrested were held temporarily in the city's Velodrome d'Hiver. They were crammed into the building, in almost suffocating heat, without any food or water.

The Goldenbergs – the Turkish parents and their ten children – were among those arrested in the roundup on Thursday, 16th July. At Drancy, Mrs Goldenberg was separated from her daughter, Sylvie, who was aged five or six. Mrs Goldenberg was one of those shipped off to a camp in a cattle train. She was never seen again. Sylvie, however, was a survivor. A German soldier slashed her face, and here we are in 2020, and Sylvie still has the scar on her cheek, a reminder of the terrors she experienced in her childhood. After four months at Drancy, she was taken in by Catholic nuns. Like many Jews during the war – and Danièle was one of them – Sylvie was baptised. She remained with the nuns, protected until the end of the war. Then she was reunited with her father. Her brothers, Albert and Simon, were also survivors. In order to live through the war, they had played on the fact that they had Turkish roots because Turkey was sympathetic to the German cause.

Of all the uncertainties during their lives at this time, Simon and Albert were certain of one thing – it was Roi who had denounced them, and led the Nazis to their door. The deaths in their family, the horrors and heartbreak they had experienced; it was Monsieur Roi, the Chilean, who betrayed them. 'There are Jews living there,' he had said to the Nazis. The two brothers swore to avenge the deaths of their parents.

It is clear that once the Goldenbergs had found Roi, he did

not live for much longer. Here, however, the story takes a twist or two. The two brothers went to the police, and told them how Roi had collaborated with the Germans. They gave his address to the police. Then they bribed the officers to interview Roi on the ground floor of the police station. 'Make sure that he is left alone for a while,' they said to the police. 'Leave the window open.'

Sure enough, Roi was arrested, taken to the police station and into a room on the ground floor, where the window was open. When Roi was left alone, he seized the chance to escape. He jumped out of the window and ran… then there was a gunshot. Or was it two or three shots? Roi was hit and he died.

Now, there are two possibilities. Either he was shot by the police under the instructions of the brothers. Or the brothers were waiting next to the station, and they shot him dead. We shall never know. Yet it is known that the brothers were the only two official suspects – Roi had been murdered and one of the brothers had killed him. But which one of them had pulled the trigger? Simon or Albert?

With the police in pursuit, the brothers went to Albert's friend, Raoul, for his help. Which, as a wise lawyer, he gave. First, Raoul used his government connections to arrange for Simon to swiftly leave France and to go to East Berlin, where nobody would be able to touch him. Simon had a criminal record, and did not fancy his chances if he stayed in Paris. Second, Raoul planned the next move for Albert. 'I want you to surrender yourself to the police,' said Raoul. 'I will come with you to the police station.' Albert, accompanied by the lawyer, handed himself in, and he was arrested and charged. Next, came the trial, at which Raoul presented his case for the defence. On grounds of contumacy, or failure to appear in court, Simon was prosecuted in absentia.

It was true, Raoul admitted, that Albert and Simon had tracked down the man who had denounced their family to the Nazis. 'If one of them is the murderer, then which one? One of them – Simon –

has escaped. And the other one – Albert – has surrendered himself to the police. Albert says he didn't do it, and there is no evidence to contradict his claim. Simon is not here to give his account to the court. He is beyond reach of the French authorities.' Raoul concluded, 'We will never know what happened.'

The verdict was a victory for the Goldenbergs. Simon was condemned in absentia to the death penalty. Provided he was not extradited (which he was not) it meant that under French law he could only be arrested and subsequently executed if he set foot on French soil within twenty-five years of being sentenced. For his part, Albert was given a jail sentence of three months, suspended. With the help of Raoul's guidance and defence, neither brother spent a day behind bars for the killing.

*

As Raoul made his way through the streets of post-war Paris, he contemplated the meeting with the lady who was seeking a divorce. Someone had recommended to her Maître Raoul Saiman. 'Go and see him, and see what he can do for you.'

She had made an appointment to meet and discuss the situation, but then Raoul had said, 'Do you know Goldenberg's restaurant in rue des Rosiers?' Albert's restaurant in the old Jewish quarter, and the one in which Raoul had a stake. 'Why not meet me there, and then we'll talk about your case.' And so, one evening shortly afterwards, Marcelle Philippon (née Boissière) arrived at Goldenberg's restaurant.

Over aperitifs with Raoul Saiman, she began to talk about her failed marriage to the pharmacist, Jean, who had left her and their daughter, Norma, and then he had left France and was now building a new life in Cambodia. 'I understand,' said Raoul, and he suggested that they finish their drinks at Goldenberg's place, and then eat supper in another restaurant. 'We can talk in the car,' said Raoul. They stubbed out their cigarettes – he smoked Camel, she smoked Lucky Strike – and finished their drinks. And they left one restaurant, and began the drive to another. Marcelle had told him so much of her own life, but Raoul had shared little of his own story. After all, he was not there to talk but mostly to listen.

All of a sudden, as Raoul and Marcelle motored through the bustling streets, an ordinary moment shifted towards an extraordinary one. Raoul's car broke down in rue Pigalle. They could walk to the restaurant, or they could hail a taxi. There was another option. 'My apartment,' said Raoul, 'is nearby. It's in Square La Bruyère. Shall we go there? We can talk over drinks.'

Five

Two Halves

So they never went to the restaurant that evening. Personal feelings got in the way of professional ethics. Instead of discussing divorce at the table, Raoul took Marcelle to his apartment. He seduced her, or maybe she seduced him. Within the subsequent months, they were making whoopee. When they had eventually got around to talking through her divorce from Jean, there was another Marcelle mess that needed to be tidied up by Raoul, with his clever mind and ability to strategise.

Norma, Marcelle's daughter, had lived with Marcelle's parents in Deauville. That is, until one day her grandmother told her, 'You have to be hidden somewhere.' And she encouraged Norma to climb into a cupboard, and then she took the cupboard to a friend's home in the countryside. Norma remembered that this was the home of 'a chubby and very nice lady', but again, how long she stayed here, she could not recall.

On a summer's day, however, in the middle of a hot afternoon, two gentlemen and a lady arrived in a large black Citroën. She would remember clearly watching on, as the adults spoke to each other. And she would remember one of the gentlemen saying to her, 'This is your grandmother.' It was Jean's mother. 'You must come with her.' Little Norma was terrified. In this one moment she had learnt that this woman – a stranger – was in fact her paternal grandmother, and that she would have to leave with her in the car. The child sobbed. She did not want to leave, and she put up a struggle when the men moved her towards the car.

They drove away. She would never forget that she was wearing only a swimsuit, and that she was not given the opportunity to change out of it and into other clothes before being taken from her maternal grandparents and into the custody of her paternal grandparents.

This was all taking place because her parents' divorce proceedings had begun. Her mother, with her lover, the lawyer Raoul, had initiated the legal action. The two gentlemen who had arrived in the Citroën were police commissioners engaged by Mme Philippon, mother of Jean. 'The dear woman, I do not blame her,' Norma would later say. 'She was acting for her son in Cambodia, because at that time my mother did not have custody rights.'

Norma adapted well to another twist of her young life. She regarded Vierzon as 'a good change of scenery'. She liked her paternal grandmother, Marthe, and got on well with her Aunt Madeleine (sister of Jean) and her husband Marcel Mabillot. When she was much older and reflected on this period, she would say, 'I did not even think I had a mother.'

*

Whether or not she had a mother did not cross Norma's mind, but then one morning grandmother Marthe said, 'Norma, your mum is coming to see you today.' It was the summer of 1948, and Norma was five years old. Shortly afterwards, Norma saw a lady arrive, and she hovered on the terrace, did not come into the house. It was

Marcelle, her mother. Again, Norma watched as the adults spoke to each other.

Then they took little Norma and they went, with the child's uncle and aunt, to a police station. There Marcelle signed some documents, essentially a declaration that she would return Norma to her grandmother. It was supposed to be a brief visit, an agreed short meeting between mother and daughter.

What happened next, Norma would recall in writing: 'I'm alone with Mum. We run at full speed to reach a car, hidden not far away. It was Raoul's 202 Peugeot, driven by Uncle Jean (Marcelle's brother).'

They drove to Paris. Norma never forgot that as they drove along, her mother told Jean, 'Luckily, I bandaged my stomach.' The bandages hid the bump from her in-laws – Marcelle was five months pregnant. When it was well past the time when Marcelle had agreed to return Norma to the Philippons, the child was arriving at her new home: Raoul's apartment at Square La Bruyère in Pigalle. To Norma, Raoul was "Raroul" because when she met him, the three-year-old found his name too difficult to pronounce correctly.

*

I was that bump behind the bandages. I was born in a clinic in rue Lauriston on 9th December 1948, the year after my parents had met in Albert Goldenberg's restaurant to talk about Marcelle's divorce. The clinic was the same one in which Norma had been born, beside what had been the Gestapo's headquarters.

I was delivered by Dr Léon Stain, my father's faithful friend and our family doctor. And Dr Stain was born in Poland, and he was named Leonovitch Stein but the war changed that. He had been a doctor in Warsaw, but had escaped the Germans. I am not sure how he met my father but, apart from delivering me, he would also tell me years later during which my father helped him to obtain a French passport which was in the new name of Léon Stain.

He also lived at my father's apartment while retaking the necessary exams to practise as a doctor in France. For my birth, Dr Stain was assisted by Madame Gauthier, the midwife who had also helped to deliver Norma.

Raoul had given Marcelle security. Marcelle had given Raoul the one thing he desperately wanted – a son. Soon I was to be known as 'Patou' (to the French, it is the common abbreviation for Patrice or Patrick). I have few memories of the early years of my life. The recollections simply are not there, or rather there are just a few things that I can recall. But far more recently, Norma and I played a game, each drawing a picture of how we remembered the apartment on the fourth floor of 2, Square La Bruyère. Our drawings were almost identical. Of the layout of the place, Norma has said to me, 'It is engraved in my memory.'

There was very large entrance with parquet flooring that was polished every morning – it had to be spick and span should Raoul's clients visit. As a toddler I would cycle my four-wheeler on the polished floor. On the right of the entrance there was a kitchen, with a huge cooler replenished by weekly deliveries of ice and bread. There was a door for the servants' entrance, where Norma would go to see Renée and Joseph, and where she grew beans between cotton wool.

There was a small room, known as the green room, which overlooked an inner courtyard, where she would see her school friend Elisabeth Momal, whose father was a doctor. 'I thought it was nice,' said Norma, 'to see them dine with their family.' Next, there was another large room. This was known as "la chambre du mileu" – the middle room. (Raoul was a Freemason and perhaps the name of this room was a nod to a traditional Freemasons' lodge, which also has a middle room or chamber.)

This middle room had three entrances: one door led to the hallway; another door led to the laundry room, where the washing machine boiled; and the third door to a corridor that was filled with big closets. It was in this room that Norma and I slept. One Christmas we made a little wooden chalet and put it on the fireplace, alongside glowing candles: a very pretty sight, but thankfully we did not set our home ablaze.

The apartment had another huge room that was home to my electric train set, installed when I was two years old. 'I can still see you,' said Norma decades later, 'flabbergasted, sucking your thumb, stroking your nose with one of your dad's silk ties.' My cot was in my parents' bedroom, and Norma would often come to put syrup on my gums to ease my teething and stop my crying. It did the trick, and calmed me down. And beside my parents' room, there was a bathroom. Norma would watch as Marcelle got ready before going out for the night. 'I still smell her perfume and her face powder.' She did not want her mother to leave, but it was good that Renée and Joseph were there to babysit.

There was a grand and beautiful dining room with windows made of tiled, coloured glass. One day Norma was in the kitchen and leant on the doors of the large kitchen cupboard and – crash! – the cupboard fell on top of her. She ran to Raoul, who was listening to music in the dining room. 'Raroul, Raroul,' she howled and she threw herself into his arms. He comforted her, and she felt accepted by him.

The dining room had considerably sized French doors which opened onto a living room, again large, with three huge windows. At Christmas, this room was the site of a beautifully decorated tree that stood beside the fireplace. The living room was also the setting for my circumcision ceremony. 'I managed to sneak between the gentlemen with their kippahs,' Norma recalled, 'and came near you, lying on a white bed. I did not understand what was happening. But you were screaming very loudly. Mum had locked herself at the other end of the apartment.' Later, this room was used for Norma's solemn communion when she was aged eleven or twelve.

Then there was my father's office within the apartment. Norma liked to go in when he wasn't around, and look at his bookcase, with its glass panels and see-through net curtains. The apartment's kitchen, I recall, was large and led to a smaller room, where there was a large thermal chamber, which was filled once or twice a week with a couple of slabs of ice. At the back of this little room was a door which led to the service staircase, which I'd climb to get to Renée and Joseph on the sixth floor.

Norma has plenty of strong memories but my own recollections, as I say, are blurry and limited. I'm not sure if I actually recollect or if I learnt to recollect. Are they real memories, or things that I have been told and they come to mind as if they are memories?

There is one memory which is still here, and I am looking at it now. It's a scar on the index finger of my right hand. Every evening I would wait for my father to return to the apartment and beside the lift I had a little chair and a table, what I called 'my desk'. The lift was the old-fashioned sort, with metal collapsible grilles for doors. Of course, these grilles were always a dangerous hazard for little fingers. One evening I put mine into the grilles as the lift was coming up. I don't know whether or not the lift stopped to open, but my index finger was injured and blood spurted from it. Obviously, I screamed in pain. My mother later told me that I was put in my white coat and then she rushed me downstairs, and to the front of the building, to catch a taxi to take us to the hospital. Suddenly my father pulled up in his car, saw the pair of us – and the blood – and then he drove us to the hospital, where I was treated and received stitches. It is not a memory that has ever faded, partly because to this day I have the scar to remind me.

There is another episode which I remember. Or one that I think that I remember, although it could have been "planted in my memory bank" by Renée and Joseph and my mother, who would later tell me the story. It is that in the footwell of my father's desk I would happily build myself a little house or den, where I spent time playing with my toys.

Our parents were socialites, and so frequently went out at night. They went to the theatre, and they both enjoyed gambling and liked to go to the casino d'Enghien, where my father taught my mother how to play baccarat. My father was a devoted admirer of classical music, and he inspired my mother to take an interest. She did more than that. Maman loved Puccini, Chopin, Vivaldi and Mozart, as well as *La Bohème, La Traviata, Madame Butterfly*.

They often spent nights at the opera, and they ate at expensive restaurants. At Chez Lassere, where my father had VIP status, they dined magnificently. The maître d' would swoon and fuss over them, and invariably at the end of the meal he would present my mother with a gift, a little copper saucepan.

Years later, Liz and I took my mother back to Lassere. I knew how special it was to her, and that my father was the first to take her there. We ate extremely well, although my mother, as usual, did not praise the food because, of course, she could have done a better job. I asked the restaurant's resident pianist to play "Roses de Picardie", my mother's favourite song. At the end of the meal, the maître d' came to the table. 'Mesdames,' he began, and he offered the ladies a small porcelain saucepan. Liz thanked him. 'How lovely,' said Liz. 'Thank you.' Then it was my mother's turn. 'My husband used to bring me here regularly after the war,' she began, 'and back then, as he was a special customer, I was always given a small toy saucepan. But it was made of copper.' She held up the mini saucepan. 'Porcelain. It's just not the same as copper.' I tried my best to demonstrate to the maître d' that his thoughtful gesture was greatly appreciated, and he smiled politely but by then the damage was done. It was embarrassing.

*

When our parents went out for the evening, Renée and Joseph were the babysitters, our guardian angels. They had been with Raoul for a long time and stayed with us, faithful and loving. To Norma and me, they were our adopted grandparents, just as they were to Danièle.

Their living arrangements may have changed a little since Danièle's days. Their quarters were still on the sixth floor, but amounted to three servants' rooms, which they shared with Renée's brother, Camille. They also had a dog, a boxer bitch. When Norma returned from her school on rue Blanche, she'd dash up the service staircase to visit them. Often, she would have lunch there, and Joseph would listen in to TSF, to catch up on news of the war in Korea. Norma was usually happy to be with them, not least because they were interested in her life, and in her collection of perfume vials which were so fashionable at the time.

As a little boy, I would crawl on all fours up the circular staircase. At one side of me there was a handrail, with supporting balusters, which looked down into the emptiness below. On the other side of me there was a stained-glass window, which looked down onto the courtyard below. However, one of the supporting balusters was missing, and a panel of stained glass was broken. I was scared that I would fall all the way down through the balustrade or on my right I would fall through the broken glass and land on the yard outside.

Then I would call out to Renée or Joseph for help. I could crawl to the top, you see, but I couldn't crawl back down the staircase. If I close my eyes, I am back there now, and calling, 'Renée! Joseph!'

And I was indeed back there. I returned a few years ago, and took along Ollie. In the building where I had lived, briefly, with my father, I now stood as a father and with my son. You know these old buildings in Paris, they never really change much and 2, Square La Bruyère is no exception. It was a weird experience and Ollie, I think, was quite moved to be there. The casing of the lift seemed different, but the staircase was just the same. The red tiles were still there. The walls alongside the stairs were still two shades of brown; light at the top, dark at the bottom.

I said to Ollie, 'Renée and Joseph lived there, at the top, and I used to climb the service staircase from the floor where we lived. Servants did not use the lift.' And I said, 'Come on...' I wanted to see if the missing baluster was still there, and if the stained glass was still broken. We got up to the sixth floor and there it was, the missing baluster. And there it was, the broken glass.

Our family went regularly to Albert Goldenberg's restaurant. Walking along in rue des Rosiers, Norma was fascinated by the Hasidic Jews with their long, curly beards and black hats, and etched in her memory is the time that she saw a Hasidic Jew carrying a recently-despatched chicken in his hand.

My father and Albert were not merely friends; they were as close as brothers. In 1951 – almost three weeks after my third birthday, and when Norma was aged eight – they had a double wedding on Thursday, 20th December. Raoul married Marcelle, and Albert married Olga, a Romanian Jew. As well as Sylvie, Albert's daughter from his first marriage, Olga also had a daughter, Jacqueline, from a previous marriage.

There we were, the happy family, and probably happier now that our mother and father were married. Later, I was proud to be known in rue des Rosiers as "le fils de Raoul", rather than Patrice.

*

Norma recalls standing in rue Cadet, outside the Grand Lodge of France, while Raoul talked to his friends. He was a Freemason, and a lawyer for the Grand Lodge. Norma bowed to the gentlemen.

She has memories, too, of standing outside the Sceaux Clinic with Raoul. Maman was inside, visiting her brother Jean. It was Jean who had driven the getaway car when they took Norma from the Philippons. Now he was bedridden, was suffering a lung disease. Norma heard the word "pneumothorax", and our mother guaranteed the clinic fees, she said, from her casino winnings. (My mother's claim that she could pay from her winnings may or may not be correct. I recall, as an adult in the mid-1970s, giving her 500 francs when she said she needed money. Later I learned that she had lost it at the casino d'Enghien.)

As a family, we went on holiday in those early years to Juan-les-Pins, in the South of France, where we stayed at the Hôtel du Midi (today it is Hôtel du Lys). Our parents would spend evenings at the famous Casino de Juan-les-Pins, and Aunt Thérèse (our mother's sister) became the babysitter. 'One night, while I was sleeping,' Norma told me, 'Thérèse took me for a walk, to see one of her lovers. But unfortunately for her she saw Raoul's car pass under the Pont du Lys and, to avoid being seen, she lifted me up and we jumped into a ditch. That's when we heard the shouts of a man – Ouille! Ouille! Ouch! Ouch! We had accidentally landed on a tramp who was trying to sleep in the ditch.' And Norma also recalls that when I was aged two or three, and we were in Juan-les-Pins, I was so ill that my father summoned Dr Stain from Paris. It is illustrative of the men's relationship. Dr Stain would do anything for my father, who had helped him to become a French citizen with a new name, and helped him to study so he could acquire his licence to practise in France.

Six

The Terrible Mistake

The suitcases were packed, and there was an air of excitement at home. 'We are going on holiday,' my mother had told Norma and me. Soon we would lock up the apartment, leave Paris and head for the South of France. Norma was approaching her tenth birthday, and I was aged four and three months. It was a holiday for us, the children, but importantly this was to be a period of recuperation for my father. That, really, was the purpose of this break in the Côte d'Azur. We would stay in the now-familiar Juan-les-Pins and – beneath a warm sun and in the sea air – my father would get well again.

At the beginning of that year, 1953, Raoul had an ear infection, a common otitis or swelling of the inner or middle ear. However, this had turned into the more serious and less common complaint, cerebrospinal meningitis. This is an inflammation of the meninges, the three layers of membranes that cover and protect the brain and spinal cord. The illness can be fatal, and Raoul was soon hospitalised. For some time he had been at a clinic around the corner from the apartment, and he was being treated by his cousin,

Professor Berrard, a surgeon. This treatment involved a succession of lumbar punctures, during which a thin, hollow needle is inserted between the bones of the lower spine to collect cerebrospinal fluid. The fluid is tested to determine whether the patient is suffering from meningitis.

This procedure, also known as a spinal tap, can be extremely painful. Most people would shudder at the prospect of having it done once, but by the end of February, my father had undergone about twenty-five lumbar punctures. After the twenty-fifth spinal tap, he was doing so well that he left the clinic and returned home.

He spent only the weekend at home, however, because of a conversation he'd had with his cousin, the surgeon. 'Raoul, everything looks good,' said Berrard. It was reassurance that every patient wants to hear from the doctor. Then Berrard added, 'But better safe than sorry. Let's do one more lumbar puncture before you go off for a break.' Meanwhile, Raoul's faithful doctor and friend, Dr Stain, was awaiting test results of the previous lumbar puncture. There was no question that my father seemed to be recovering, but these results would establish the state of Raoul's meningitis.

Apart from his health, Raoul had another concern. My mother and Danièle argued often, and their rows bothered my father. Danièle could be volatile and forthright, and, like my mother, she was her own person. When these two strong personalities clashed, the hostility was stressful for my father and had escalated to the point of driving him crazy. He pleaded for them to improve their relationship.

One day Danièle's visit to the clinic coincided with my mother's arrival. As they were together, Raoul had grabbed the opportunity to say to them, 'Can you both promise me you will try to get on with each other? Please.' They both promised.

*

And so there was a plan to follow regarding my father's treatment. After his weekend at home, Raoul would go back to the clinic for one more lumbar puncture and then, on the Tuesday, 3rd March, he would come back to the apartment. The Peugeot would be loaded up with our luggage, so we'd be ready to go, beginning the drive southwards to Juan-les-Pins, a journey of about ten hours.

On that Tuesday morning, my father had prepared himself so that he could leave the clinic as soon as possible after the procedure. He didn't want to waste any more time. He had shaved and put on his watch. He did not want to forget it, and time was on his mind. Raoul was well-organised and, on this occasion, he was eager to escape the city and to be with his family.

The spinal tap procedure took place, the large needle being inserted into Raoul's spine and fluid extracted. After the lumbar puncture, he was supposed to lie flat on the bed. However, a nurse found him sitting upright, though hunched, on his bed. Shortly afterwards, my father died.

At our home, my mother was busily preparing for the days ahead, the drive southwards, and the family holiday beyond. She was doing the last bits of packing, the final moments of tidying. Ordinary stuff. And then the telephone call from the clinic. 'Madame Saiman' – she was always so proud to be Madame Saiman, the wife of the powerful lawyer – 'Madame Saiman. Je suis desolé… vraiment…' The dreadful news was delivered. Her husband, my father, Norma's step-father, Danièle's father; the seemingly invincible Salomon Raoul Saiman, survivor of World War II, and a gun attack at short range when he was thirty, had died. He was fifty-three years old.

Our mother – shocked, panicked, fearful – quickly left the apartment and rushed to the nearby clinic. But she was not there long when Dr Stain arrived, and they saw each other. He had a broad smile, a cheerful look in his eyes. In fact, he seemed ecstatic, and before she could speak, he declared, 'Marcelle! Marcelle! I've had the test results. It's fantastic news.'

'*Raoul est guéri. Il est guéri.*' Raoul is cured. He's cured. He's going to be fine.

*

We would never know precisely how Raoul died. There may have been an air bubble in the needle, or some other mistake during the procedure. But as I say, we never knew, and we never will. So I was left with the notion, if you like, that my father died when effectively he was no longer ill. It was the worst sort of mistake, the most terrible accident.

My mother, years later, would tell me a story about that day. My father's body was being taken from the hospital to be brought home, when the receptionist reminded my mother that the bill had to be settled when a patient left. My mother, in her typical style, responded, 'Probably when a patient leaves, but not a cadaver.'

But I remember nothing of that day, nothing of that period in my life. Norma has a recollection of the two of us, standing in the middle room, with a view into my parents' bedroom. Norma could see the body of "Raroul", there on the bed, with people gathered at his bedside. And then Norma and I were moved to one side, perhaps by Renée or Joseph, so that we no longer had the view of sadness and grief.

My half-sister Danièle was now an orphan in her mid-twenties. She was infuriated by a group from the Jewish community. They gathered around my father, dressed in his best suit, and were muttering away in Hebrew. 'My father did not speak a word of Hebrew,' she said. 'Get out.' Which was very brave.

After the funeral, Danièle was asked to leave the flat that my father had found for her. 'Your father has died,' said the owner, 'so now can you get out of the apartment.' It turned out that my father's last request had been for Danièle and my mother to stop their fighting. They did indeed do their best to get along. (They remained mostly civil to each other, and they stayed in touch, although in later life I invited the two of them for lunch and my mother could not resist saying to Danièle, 'You were not a very clean teenager and you left your dirty clothes everywhere.' My mother never escaped her childhood concerns of cleanliness.)

When I was older and inquired about my father's funeral, I was told that I was not taken along. I don't know why I was not taken, but I wasn't. As mourners gathered at the Jewish cemetery to bid farewell to my father, I was at home, being looked after by Renée and Joseph. When I consider the love and respect my father had for this couple, it seems strange that they, too, were not at his funeral.

Did my mother ever tell my father about her wartime love affair with the German commandant? I do not know the answer, but I do wonder if she would have dared ruin her chances with Raoul by confessing to the relationship.

*

As I have no primary recollections of my father, there are of course no memories of affection between us. I do not remember him cuddling me. I do not recall those moments when he kissed me goodnight, or read to me or sang to me a lullaby. I do know, through Danièle and Norma, that he doted on me. I do know that he used to call me '*mon coco chéri*', my darling coconut.

I was never able to call my father "Papa", and much later on when talking to Danièle or to Patricia it was quite strange that I would not say "Papa" when talking about him. Interestingly enough, the Jews only refer in writing to "G_d", and never "God". Even more strangely, while my mother would talk to me about my father, she would always refer to him rather formally as "ton père" and never "ton papa", which might have been more appropriate.

It was mostly through Renée and Joseph that I was able to learn more about my father. They could tell me about his life before the War, and Danièle could tell me about his relationship with Henriette, Danièle's mother and Raoul's first wife. I was told about his love for the opera, and how moved he was as he listened on a record, or watched from the audience. 'When he listened to the opera,' said Danièle, 'he would be in tears.' There are very few operas at which I don't cry. Like my father, I am frequently moved by music.

I do have to accept that I never really knew my father, and don't remember him. From a few photographs, I established a picture of my father in my mind's eye: a man, not impressively attractive, wearing glasses and showing signs of baldness. There were many photographs which were in my father's briefcase (which was lost), along with piles of telegrams.

One of the things which I had to accept is – well, no, I have never accepted – the fact that my mother did not keep more photographs. All I have today is just five, six or seven photographs of my father and me. They are what I have been left finally.

Every picture tells a hundred stories, they say. There is a photograph of my father and me. We are looking up to the sky. The photograph was taken outside Albert Goldenberg's deli, in rue des Rosiers.

Shortly before my father went into hospital, we went to Parc Monceau. I have another picture of my father and me in that same park, and it is possibly the last-ever photograph of my father. We went perhaps for a family outing, a Sunday stroll through the beautiful gardens. It's a wintry day; the trees are bare, and my smartly dressed father is wearing an overcoat. Norma is nearby, skipping and smiling. I am standing in front of my father, smiling and looking towards the photographer (who must have been my mother).

There was a man who was selling balloons, and my father bought one for me. '*Voici, mon coco chéri.*' He handed me the balloon, a balloon on a string. And the inevitable happened.

47

Accidentally, I let go of the string and – whoosh. The balloon sailed away, heavenwards, unreachable, uncatchable. To any young child, it would have been confusing, upsetting. An early experience of loss, if you like. Norma, who would have been nine years old, later told me, 'You were very upset to lose that balloon.'

The confusion that comes with loss must have returned some weeks later. This time I had not lost a balloon. I had lost my father. '*Où est Papa?*' Where is Daddy?

My mother said, 'Your father has gone to the sky to get the balloon.'

In 1953, the year that my father died and when I lost the balloon in the park, the French director and cinematographer Albert Lamorisse began work on what would be his fourth short film. It was entitled *Le Ballon Rouge* – The Red Balloon – and would be released to great acclaim in 1956. The silent film told the story of Pascal, a five-year-old Parisian – he was, in fact, played by Lamorisse's son, Pascal – who finds a red balloon and makes friends with it. Pascal loses the balloon and it floats up, up and away. Pascal chases it through the streets of Paris, frequently looking up to his friend in the sky, and then there are a few nasty kids who destroy it.

Le Ballon Rouge won numerous awards, including a Palme d'Or at the Cannes Film Festival, and an Oscar for best original screenplay. The film was accompanied, in the following year, by the publication of a book of the same name. It was a picture book, featuring still photographs from the film and with a narrative written by Lamorisse. Both as film and book, *The Red Balloon* touched a global audience of all ages. In these post-war years, the bright red balloon was a symbol of hope above the grey and partly demolished backdrop of Paris. The film, said Jean Cocteau, was 'a fairy tale without fairies'.

As a child, I owned the book, and strangely – because perhaps of the episode in the park, and because of what my mother had said about my father's possible reappearance – that balloon conveyed the same message: a symbol of hope, that my father might return, that he might possibly come back from the sky with *le ballon*.

A few years ago I was in Paris, and had been thinking about *Le Ballon Rouge*. I am not sure what reminded me of the book, although perhaps, in truth, it has never been far from my mind. I decided to phone around the vintage bookshops, to see if one of them had an original copy. 'Yes, we have a couple,' said a voice at the other end of the phone. 'I'll put a copy to one side for you.' So, off I went, to a bookshop in Saint-Germain. I bought the book and there was a part of me thinking, this is crazy, sixty-five years after my father's death.

That evening, and in my hotel room, I lay on my bed, took the book and began to read. I was only a few pages in when the memory came back to me, the memory of my mother saying, 'Your father has gone to get the balloon.' I felt tears well up, and very soon I was overwhelmed by waves of emotion, sobbing like a child, crying my eyes out.

Seven

A Chalet in the Alps

'Papa has gone to the sky to get your balloon.' Would this be the explanation I would give to a boy, a little over four years old, who has just lost his father? What I thought at the time, I don't know. What I feel as an adult today is that it does not show empathy. It's not what I would have said to a young child. There's a chance that it might have made me feel some guilt about my father's disappearance: had I not let go of the balloon, he wouldn't have needed to leave to retrieve it. I have never felt guilty about it, but even so.

I believe that at the time of my father's death, my mother went to pieces. She could only think about her own loss, and this meant that she did not have the capacity to think of me or, for that matter, anyone else.

Around that time, I have a foggy memory, again involving loss. I liked to sleep with my mother, on my father's side of the bed. That is where I was lying and beside me was a canary, our little yellow pet which lived in a gilded cage. It was a sunny morning and the bedroom window was open. I wanted to hold the bird, and so I opened the cage door. Whoosh! The bird flew from behind its bars out into the room, towards the window and then, that was it, gone… I was a stupid boy, maybe, but heartbroken.

Within a month of my father's death, Norma and I were sent to stay with my mother's brother, Jean, and his pregnant wife, Yolande. Uncle Jean and Aunt Yolande lived in Vaujours, a village about an hour and a half away, in the suburbs of north-east Paris. While our mother got on with fixing her life in Paris, Norma and I spent five or six months here. We lived above a café which, I think, was owned by Yolande's parents.

Here in this little village, many of my earliest memories seemed to have been formed. I remember walking through the streets, and the village tailor, who was amiable and chatty, gave me some chocolate. I remember, too, being bitten by a dog on my way home from school. And I remember that Norma and I slept in the same bed; there was a curtain in the room, and on the other side there was Jean and Yolande's bed. One night I vomited on Norma's back – an overdose of chocolate, perhaps, courtesy of the tailor. Norma was not pleased and had to have a shower in the middle of the night. Uncle Jean had inherited Raoul's Peugeot 202 – the car was not left in a will, our mother gave it to him. I enjoyed sitting in the back of the car because in Vaujours it was the only thing I had left of my father.

When we returned to Paris, Renée and Joseph did their best to boost our spirits. Sometimes we would go to their quarters a couple of floors above us, and Renée would make a feast of pancakes, and they would talk to me about my father, as I sat and listened, entranced. This kind married couple was the backbone of my stability.

I would busy myself in the footwell of my father's desk, building a den for *mon nounours*, my teddy bear. One day I made a parachute for my bear: I took a towel, made holes in the middle. I attached four strings to the towel, and to my bear. Now he had his own parachute! I leant on a window sill in the bedroom at the end of the corridor, and launched bear plus parachute into the Paris air. I watched as – boosh! – he plummeted to the ground. That was not expected. Then I went down the stairs and got my bear. His injuries, considering, were minimal: one glass eye broken in half. The experiments ceased.

I attended a school in rue Blanche, though only briefly. Although there was an increase in the number of tuberculosis cases in France during the war (partly due to mass movement of the population, as people fled the Nazis), the mortality rate had since fallen. The BCG is the vaccine against TB, and was designed by two French bacteriologists (Albert Calmette and Camille Guérin, who named the product Bacillus Calmette-Guérin).

However, my BCG injection failed, apparently. This bothered my mother, and she explained that it would be best for me to move for a while from Paris to the fresh air of the French Alps, where she had found a home for young people who were also vulnerable to the disease. Tuberculosis is highly contagious, and in the past sufferers were put into a home, or sanatorium. And so, shortly after Christmas 1956 – about a month after I had turned seven – that is where I went. My mother took me by train to Grenoble. (We travelled with another boy and his mum, who my mother had previously met.) From Grenoble station, we took the bus to the chalet that was in the snowy Alpine town of Villard-de-Lans. Over several decades this area had established itself as "a cure village", with convalescent homes and sanatoria especially for children. Sometimes families would come and stay in such homes. Not in my case: I was to be left alone.

My mother left and… well, I just got on with life, really. I was put in a dormitory with other boys, and I liked the friendship, the camaraderie. There was also a routine which, looking back, gave me security. After breakfast every morning, we'd ski down the big slope beside the chalet. These days skiing is quite easy: slip into your boots and buckle a few catches, pick up your lightweight, fibreglass skis and off you go. Back then, the boots had to be laced and the skis were wooden and, particularly to a six-year-old, they were heavy. There was no such thing as a chair lift in those days, so we'd ski down and then trudge back up the slope, panting as we lugged our skis and sledges. But it was quite enjoyable, and with plenty of snowball fighting. After lunch, we'd sleep for an hour in the afternoon, and then we'd have school lessons. There was lots of playtime, and drawing times tables with crayons; these were pinned on the walls, which made us feel proud. And then we ate dinner, followed by bed, lights out, sleep and wake up to do it all over again the following day.

Thinking about that experience, I would say it was perfect inasmuch as it was regular – as a child, I knew what to expect and what I was getting, and there were no ugly surprises to upset or confuse me.

There were weekly events. I remember, for instance, that on Saturdays the chalet owner (or maybe she was the manageress) would take me by the hand and together we would walk to the market place in Villard-de-Lans. She'd always stop and speak to the town's mayor. He was quite a large man, and at the time I thought he was just a friend of hers. He may have been a bit more than a friend, I'll never know. But again, I liked the regularity of these walks into town, and it felt lovely to hold someone's hand.

And then, every Thursday we would all sit down and write letters home. In other words, once a week from my arrival at the chalet until August of the same year, I would write a letter to my mother in Paris. That means she would have received about twenty-five letters from me. I genuinely wish I could remember receiving a single letter from my mother. I do not. I cannot remember whether she wrote to me, or did not write to me. I do not remember getting a letter from her, but equally I do not recall being upset not to have received a letter from her. So ideally, I would like to say that I did receive letters but, alas, I cannot.

What I do know is that for eight months she never came to see me. Maybe the home had said something along the lines of, 'If you come for a weekend it's disturbing for the children.' Possibly. The question I ask myself is: if I were in my mother's position, would I have considered not seeing my child? I would go to see the child, whether it is once every three weeks, or whatever. Yes, I would go to see my child. But she did not come. My mother did not come to see me, but I do not remember having a feeling that I was missing her.

It is true that our mother had removed Norma and me from the madness that may have followed Raoul's death. It is unlikely she could have looked after us, she would not have been able to cope, and that sending us away from home was a life-saving exercise. Saving whose life? All of ours, perhaps.

Eight

Maurice, the Secret

As Maurice Rignault arrived at the Hôtel de Béthune-Sully, one of the most beautiful private mansions in Paris, he gave himself perhaps a moment or two to look at the seventeenth-century building and its exquisitely designed gardens. Situated in rue Saint Antoine, in the heart of the Marais, Hôtel Sully is just a few minutes' walk from the place where my father liked to spend so much of his life – Albert Goldenberg's restaurant in rue des Rosiers.

The townhouse was built in the 1620s, and was home to King Henri IV's minister, Maximilien de Béthune, Duke of Sully. The duke's best-known moment in history? In 1614 Henri was on his way to see Sully when suddenly Francois Ravaillac leapt inside the king's coach, wielding a knife. Ravaillac stabbed the monarch between the second and third ribs. The assassin paid a gruesome price: he was pulled apart by four horses going in different directions.

Since 1967 it has been the headquarters of Centre des Monuments Nationaux, having been acquired by the government in the 1950s. And it was in the 1950s, one day in the spring of 1953 to be exact, that Maurice arrived at this building, and whether he saw her, I do not know. But I know that she saw him.

Marcelle Saiman, my mother, was crossing rue St Antoine when her eyes were drawn to Maurice. She was struck by the stranger's physical appearance, just as the commandant, Salffner had been drawn to Marcelle's beauty when he saw her steal the apple in the market of Deauville years earlier.

'I saw a very attractive man with white hair,' my mother would later say, referring to Maurice, 'going into Hôtel de Sully.' It was true that Maurice was white-haired, but, now in his early forties, he still retained a full head of hair, as well as an athletic build, acquired partly through judo. Maurice was a black belt in the martial art, and quite proud of the achievement, too.

Marcelle was on her way to see a lawyer. The death of Raoul necessitated a meeting with a lawyer: his estate needed to be sorted out. And so she had made an appointment on the advice of a friend, in much the same way she had met Raoul through a recommendation. 'Go and see Maître so-and-so. He will help you deal with the estate.' Marcelle entered Hôtel de Sully and walked two storeys up the stairs, and arrived at the office, where she was greeted by a secretary.

'Bonjour Madame.'

'Bonjour. J'ai rendez-vous avec Maître...'

And then she was shown into the lawyer's office. He stood to welcome her. I do not know if at that point he found her attractive, although it's fair to say that most people considered my mother to be an extremely beautiful woman. I do know, however, that at that point she found him attractive because he was the white-haired gentleman who had caught her attention outside Hôtel de Sully, as she was crossing the street.

How long it took for their affair to begin, I do not know either. But it did begin in 1953, with my father's death a fresh memory, and it continued for nine years. And it was indeed an affair – Maurice was married. He had no children, although in time he would come to be quite fatherly towards Norma and me, as well as financially supportive of my mother and us. For some time, however, his presence remained a secret. Norma and I were completely unaware of his existence, let alone that in our mother's heart he had replaced my father, Norma's "Raroul".

*

My mother visited the chalet in Villard-de-Lans on two occasions. On the first occasion, which was at the beginning of 1956, she dropped me off, and then she took the train home to Paris. On the second occasion – eight months later, in August 1956 – she came to the chalet to collect me. She would later tell her friends, 'You know, Patrice was so happy at that home. When I picked him up, he said to me, "When can I go back to the home?" He loved it so much.' She was genuinely proud that I'd been happy there. Perhaps she was reassured that she had done the right thing.

On board the train from Grenoble to Paris, my mother told me with her characteristic directness, 'I have sold the apartment.' I tried to take in the news that our home – my father's apartment – was, in fact, no longer our home. And then she said, 'We have a new one.' I had been looking forward to being back in my father's flat, but, back in Paris, my mother took me to the newly acquired apartment on the second floor of 10, bis Avenue des Gobelins. This avenue takes its name, incidentally, from Le Manufacture des Gobelins, a tapestry factory created under the impetus of Henri IV, about a decade before he received that fatal knife blow between his second and third ribs.

The apartment was on the third floor, with a long corridor of parquet flooring, with a loo on the right and, further up, my mother's bedroom with the double bed and a window overlooking a yard. Continuing along the corridor on the right, there was the kitchen, which was opposite the dining room – home to my father's carved dining table and large hand-carved cupboard. At the end was a red armchair which opened up to become a single bed for Norma. A window overlooked the main courtyard, and there was a small door on the left that led to the bathroom.

Sometimes I shared the single bed with Norma, and later I preferred to sleep with my mother in her bed. I would sleep in my mother's bed until I was twelve years old. During those years I had night terrors, and used to sleepwalk. I had a recurring nightmare of being engulfed in a wave of green mud.

My mother had not only sold my father's apartment, but also auctioned most of his possessions within it. When subsequently I discovered how much had gone, it was as if I had lost everything. She had kept, however, the long antique dining table which had occupied the dining room of our previous home. There was also his briefcase, yet to be lost. It contained his shoes, a packet of cigarettes, and telegrams. His medals had disappeared.

It was good to be reunited with Norma, and the three of us took a train south, to Provence. My mother had a rented a villa called Villa Escapadou in the hills of Le Lavandou, and we would spend the rest of August in this pretty beach-side town. I was happy to be reunited with Norma, playing on the beach, swimming, picking grapes from vineyards, and enjoying evening meals on the terrace, looking out to sea.

Our mother had not told us about Maurice, but there is every chance she saw him during that family holiday. You see, it just so happened that Maurice had an apartment in Hyères, half an hour's drive from Le Lavandou. I don't remember seeing Maurice in that period, but suspect the choice of holiday had something to do with the proximity of Maurice.

It became apparent that it was useful for Norma and me to be away from Paris, to be away from our mother. Our absence had given her the opportunity to find a new lover, or to build a solid relationship with a lover, albeit a married man. She had once told Norma and me, '*Trouver quelq'un avec deux enfants a charge, c'est pas facile.*' It's difficult to find someone when you have two children to look after. And when she said "find", she meant "search for" – you only find when you search. For our mother, life without a man was unbearable and unthinkable.

Maurice did not have children with his wife, and maybe his relationship with my mother satisfied his desire to have a family. My mother kept letters from Maurice, and they have ended up with me. I was just flicking through the letters, which are faintly browned and speckled by time. They show a man who was deeply in love with my mother, but who says he would not divorce, citing his Catholicism. The letters also reveal Maurice as quite a jealous man, and uncertain of my mother, as one of the letters refers to other men being around my mother. He hoped, for instance, that she would remember him while she was on holiday. (Ironic, yes, that Maurice the adulterer gave lessons to my mother about fidelity.) He tended to finish his letters by asking, 'How are the children?' In one letter, he described me as 'trop bavard' – a bit too talkative.

When we returned to Paris after the summer holidays, my mother announced that she had found a boarding school for me, and I was to start there in September. This school was close to Norma's boarding school in the Vallée de Chevreuse, the natural park not far from Paris. Maman tried to present the way in which it would work: 'You and Norma will be able to take the train together on Monday mornings. From there, the bus will drop Norma at her school and then it'll take you to your school.'

I was not at all happy at the boarding school. The early Monday morning departure from home in Paris was a particularly gruelling start to the week. I hated the school breakfast, which included coffee that had skin on its surface formed by the use of whole milk. I feel nauseous just thinking back to that disgusting, wrinkly, milk skin. I refused to play with the other children in the courtyard, and yearned for Fridays when the bus would drop me outside Norma's school. With the girls, I'd play *ballon aux prisonniers*, which I suppose was the forerunner to dodgeball as it consisted of two teams trying to hit each other with a ball – once you're hit, you're out. Apart from that, my time at boarding school was in no way pleasant. As the weeks progressed, I began to slip into what I believe was probably depression. Though I can only see that now, and depression was not a common term back in those days when people had to put on a brave face and get on with life.

I refused to work at school and, within a couple of months of starting, I had finished. I was taken back home. To this day, I do not know whether the boarding school decided that I was not quite right to be there, or if my mother decided it was the wrong place for me. Fact is, I was back home and needed to find a new school.

Norma continued at boarding school, returning home for weekends. Her best friend at school was Chantale Devries, whose father, Gerald Devries, was successful in the film business. He dubbed English-speaking films into French. This craft requires writing French lines that can be delivered in perfect time to the movement of the actors' mouths on screen. (Gerald's credits included *Platoon*, *Le Tambour de Schondendoerffer* and *L'Empire des Sens*). More interestingly perhaps, during the war Gerald was a senior editor at *Paris-Soir*, the French publication that became the mouthpiece of the Nazis in Occupied France.

Meantime I started at the primary school in rue de l'Arbalète, in the fifth arrondissement, and a fifteen-minute walk from home, going up la rue Monge. I was joining in the middle of the term and the teacher, Mr Kalfakis (obviously of Greek descent), told one of the boys to give me some exercise books. '*Donne les cahiers à cet individu.*' The word *individu* translates as bloke or character, and I ended up in tears, and was crying when I walked through the front door after my first day. My mother came to the school and saw the headmaster and, while I am sure there was no apology, the matter was settled as far as I was concerned.

It was at this school that my business career began, when I was aged eight, or maybe nine. We were given stamps at school and told that we had a month to sell them. The proceeds would go to charity. I got as many stamps as possible from the teacher. Then I asked old ladies to buy the stamps from me. Which, very kindly, they did. I started splashing out, spending the money on cakes and petit choux, which I'd give as presents to my friends. The world was sweet, until the teacher asked for the money that we had received through the sales of stamps. I had spent all of it.

'I need the money, please,' I begged my mother. From memory, it was Maurice who gave me the cash and saved me a punishment at school.

Nine

❧

Claude

Throughout my school years in Paris my best friend was Claude Lurati. What I especially admired, and envied, about Claude was that he had genuine stability – he had a father and a mother, and a younger sister, Mimi. Claude had assuredness in his life. I was never quite sure what was coming next, but he knew precisely where he stood. We weren't only schoolmates. Claude lived in the same apartment block, in a flat on the other side of the inner courtyard.

Our friendship had begun at that primary school, Ecole de l'Arbalète, where we were both good pupils. It was a feeder school for Lycée Henri IV, the historic and highly prestigious secondary school in place du Panthéon, in the heart of the city's Latin quarter, and on the left bank of the Seine. Claude and I joined the lycée in 1959, at about the age of eleven, and I remained there until April 1962.

I can remember the first day at the lycée. It was scary, having to line up in what appeared to be a massive playground, and then the idea of different classes with different teachers, as well as having to change classrooms at the end of each lesson. How strange and intimidating it was, but my friendship with Claude helped to alleviate the fear that comes with being new to a school.

In the mornings, Claude and I walked to school, chattering almost incessantly about football. We were soccer mad. We walked home at lunchtime, and then walked back to the lycée for afternoon lessons, before making our way back to our flats at the end of the school day. Our route took us past the food market at rue Mouffetard, which is mostly pedestrianised.

When Rodin was our age he lived here, in this street. First thing in the morning, the market was an exhilarating spectacle of hustle and bustle as the stallholders dressed their stalls with pyramids of vegetables and fruits, mountains of cheese, huge cuts of charcuterie, and tables of ice adorned with glistening-fresh fish. The market was the hub of the community, with housewives gathering to chat and gossip, as they sniffed and squeezed fruit and vegetables before bartering. At lunchtime, when we walked home, the whole street was swallowed up by the delicious, comforting aromas of chickens as they roasted on spits, *les poulets à l'estragon*. After lunch the stallholders would close for the afternoon and, when we finished school, we'd see them getting ready to re-open for the evening.

At the bottom of rue Mouffetard, there was quite a large square in front of Saint-Médard church. Here, various sellers of kitchenware and kitchen gadgets would gather to demonstrate and show off their goods. They'd do a bit of cooking, crack a few jokes, and ask the housewives to taste the food, or check out the marvellous gadgets they were selling. (About a decade later and in Britain, I was to become one of those guys, selling non-stick pans, ironing board covers "guaranteed for life", fountain pens, pomanders for protecting clothes, invisible clothes repairs and incredibly cheap, so-called Polaroid sunglasses.)

Three teachers at the lycée were memorable. Monsieur Duvet, the French master, looked very old and he smoked with a cigarette holder that had Sellotape wrapped around it. He sat at a desk which was on a little platform at the front of the class, thereby enabling him to watch his pupils from above, like the king before his subjects. In the early days of the first term, we were asked to buy specific books for the year, and from his desk on the platform Monsieur Duvet called me up. He asked me to show him the book I had bought. It was not the right book, and I asked him, '*J'espère que ça va aller...*' I hope this will do.

The answer was a sharp backhand slap on my face.

'*Je ne suis pas ton pote.*' I am not your mate.

I think Monsieur Duvet simply wanted to send a message to the whole class: this is the way things are going to work around here. It was an experiment, and he happened to use me as the guinea pig. That was a scary message for me and my eleven-year-old classmates. Clearly, French lessons were not going to be fun. We all behaved. And guess what? At the end of the first term I received the first prize from Monsieur Duvet, and became his favourite pupil. Even better, he lived in rue Mouffetard, so from time to time Claude and I would walk to school with him and ensure that we'd have an interesting topic to chat about; something sure to ingratiate ourselves with him.

The English teacher, Monsieur Perrier, was another smoker, far younger than M. Duvet, and always dressed very smartly, usually in an impeccable suit. He sold me English, and I became a top student. The teacher for geography and history was also an author, and gave us a list of essential books to buy. They were written by him, though I cannot recall his name. He instilled within me an interest in geography and history, which I still have today. As for maths, I was not very good but Claude excelled. It's time to confess: much of my maths homework was done by Claude.

When we weren't talking about football, Claude and I were usually playing it. I was so crazy about soccer that whenever we went to see a match at Parc des Princes, the capital's giant stadium,

I'd pack my football kit and take it along with me. I did this because I hoped – I dreamed – that one day there would be an announcement on the loudspeaker: 'We are missing a player. Has anybody in the crowd got their kit?' At that point I would be able to jump up, to join the team on the pitch. There never was such an announcement, but we are all allowed to dream, aren't we?

Claude and I joined the Henri IV football team, and every Thursday, there we were – on the pitch in our kit of yellow jersey, black shorts, yellow and black socks – playing against other schools at the Stade Pershing, an old stadium with lots of football pitches. Claude and I played football in the courtyard of our apartment building, and we used garage doors as goals – scoring meant hitting the steel doors with the ball, a loud rattling bang that infuriated the concierge who complained regularly. We also drew goalposts with chalk on the walls on the inner courtyard. This annoyed the neighbours, especially as we commentated, cheered and shouted as we played. The concierge would chase us up the staircase and grumble to our parents. I cannot remember my mother or Claude's parents being bothered about it.

Other football games were indoors, like the one in the corridor of Claude's flat, with a ball made of rolled-up socks. One of us would be the goalkeeper and the other the striker, and we'd hit the ball as much as we could, pausing only to devour the fabulous crêpes made by Claude's mother. We played football with balloons, and football puce, the tiddlywink game, either in our separate flats, keeping records of games, or playing the important games together, using lamps as floodlights. I just had a look on the internet to remind myself of the pleasures of football puce, and have decided to buy myself a new set. I'll try to play with my grandchildren, and beat them.

We created puppet theatres with cardboard boxes and our audience comprised Claude's mother and his sister, Marie-Hélène (known as Mimi). Claude and I made a "telephone line", using an extremely long piece of string with two empty (and cleaned) food cans attached at either end. The line stretched right across the courtyard, from Claude's first-floor bedroom window to our bathroom window on the second floor. If either of us needed to make a call, we'd simply pull the string which, in turn, rattled the can against the other's window, and that was the telephone bell.

*

Flitting from the fun subject of football to the less fun topic of religion, Claude and I were about eleven when we began catechism. Our religious studies took place once a week in an annexe behind Saint-Médard church. Once a week we had to go to confession, which would allow us afterwards to have Sunday communion. Not to have confession meant that we'd burn in hell. Which is a pretty nasty thought for any eleven-year-old.

So every Saturday we went to confess our sins but beforehand we'd have a think about what we could tell the priest. *Stole a franc from my mother's purse... Ate some bread before my lunch which would spoil my appetite...* I was only young, but I must now confess that I made up some sins to confess to the priest. The usual punishment was two *prières*, one *notre père*, and a *Je vous salue Marie* to be repeated two or three times. Sunday mass was in Latin, and concluded with communion. The idea was not to sin between Saturday confession and Sunday mass.

Before our first holy communion (in 1961, I think) at the Sacre Coeur, we had to spend a week at a retreat with priests. This took place somewhere in the countryside, and the daily schedule required prayers in the morning, afternoon and evening, and lessons about Catholicism. There were a few games of football with priests who, weirdly, darted around the pitch in their robes. Football meets religion. After that week we had a communion procession at the Sacre Coeur, to which parents were invited. We looked quite splendid, dressed in white robes, and I was photographed so that I could forever treasure the picture (but the photo, of course, was lost).

There was a celebratory lunch at home when I was given a missal, a book containing every good Catholic's essential prayers and chants. It is also traditional to be given non-religious presents, and I was delighted to receive a new football that was on a net attached to strings. This meant I could walk with it while kicking it. A week after my First Holy Communion, we went to catechism and the priest asked all of us, 'What's the best thing that happened to you at your communion?'

I replied honestly, 'Father, the best present I got was a new football.' To this day I don't know if he thought I was taking the piss (I was not). But a slap round the face showed me it was the wrong answer. The right answer would have been: receiving Jesus. I was done with religion and never needed to go back to church or to confession. Was my answer deliberate? I don't think so. I was honest about it but obviously had not been touched by the guardian angel of advice.

At about the age of twelve, I joined a photography club which was organised by a teacher, and I stayed for a couple of years. I had a Kodak camera and took copious black and white photos, which we developed in a small, strange-smelling dark room. On one occasion I was part of a group that the teacher took to Le Havre, to see the famous ocean liner, *Le France*. For some reason, I climbed the steps and found myself on the ship, so I took photos, and then, from the top deck, proudly waved at the scowling teacher and my fellow pupils. If memory serves me well, the teacher didn't seem very happy, but maybe he thought he had lost me. Anyway, I looked at the history of *Le France* and although I did not know it then, it was a famous ship inaugurated by de Gaulle.

Those years, from 1957 to 1962, (from primary school and then at the Lycée Henri IV) formed the most stable period of my childhood, due in part to my mother's happy relationship with Maurice and my cheerful, soccer-crazy friendship with Claude. Playing games, playing football, roller skating down l'Avenue des Gobelins. Life was almost normal, and at its most stable.

Ten

The Papa Lie

Maurice had become an established fixture in our lives. Maman, clever and crafty, had even befriended his secretary. My mother trusted this woman, who helped to enable the practicalities of the affair. When Maurice and Maman fancied get-togethers, the secretary was their go-between and could keep a secret.

Of course, Maman could not *live* with Maurice. As he was a married man, their rendezvous were restricted. They had what we know in France as "cinq-à-sept": a relationship squeezed into the hours between five and seven; sex that takes place between finishing work in the office and returning to the marital home. Usually, when I returned from school the curtains were drawn. My mother would emerge from her bedroom, looking quite flushed, hair ruffled, lipstick smudged; you get the picture. 'Maurice and I are sleeping at the moment so don't disturb us,' she'd say. Happy lady.

Eventually, Maurice would come out of the bedroom and soon he was gone, heading home to his wife. Maybe it would have been best if I hadn't come home to the drawn curtains, the flushed faces.

Perhaps it would have been best if I had not been there to interrupt and to be judgemental.

I lived a lie. I was unable to tell any of my friends that my father had died. So I would imagine Maurice as my father, and I would tell friends, 'My dad's a lawyer.' This did not seem to be such an awful lie because my father had been a lawyer. There were times when I was out, walking with my mother and Maurice, and I'd see a friend coming towards me. I would go between Maurice and my mother, and hold their hands. The next day, I'd say to my friend, 'Oh, I was with my parents.' I could not bring myself to tell anybody that my father had died and, as I have said, my life was as stable as it could possibly be.

On Thursdays, and during my school-break, I would meet my mother and Maurice for lunch. Norma would come too, if she was home from boarding school. These lunches always took place in a large brasserie that was in the basement of Le Palais de Justice. I'd either walk or take the bus from Lycée Henri IV. Accessed via huge, cobbled steps at the main – and majestic – entrance of the palace, the restaurant was to my young eyes an exhilarating piece of theatre, a ballet in which the costumes reflected two grand professions: waiters in their starched white bib aprons, barristers in their long, black robes, all of them dashing here and there in the hustle, bustle of the service.

Tables were covered with paper tablecloths, and the menu was typical of the time: carotte râpée, oeuf mayonnaise, salade Niçoise, steak haché, tournedos, omelettes and, of course, frites, frites, frites. Maurice's lawyer friends would come over to our table. '*Ah, Maurice. Ça va?*' And then each of them would cast an eye around the table, smiling warmly at what they may have – must have – presumed were Maurice's wife and son (and daughter, when Norma was home from boarding school). We were not introduced by Maurice as his wife and children, but who could have blamed his colleagues for thinking that we were a strong family unit? And where was his real wife? Chez Rignault.

At every one of our Thursday lunches, I'd cheerfully devour the same three courses, starting with oeuf en gelée, followed by foie de veau avec oignons, and I finished the meal with mystère au chocolat. Then it was, '*L'addition, s'il vous plaît*', and *au revoir* before Maurice returned to court, and Marcelle went home to prepare the evening meal, and I walked or bussed it back to school.

Monday was Maman's day with Maurice. Usually she spent the weekend at home, never changing out of her dressing gown, but preparing herself for her lover. She would do the washing and, transforming herself into a vision of beauty, she'd wash her hair, do her nails and the essential *se faire des mises en plis avec des bigoudis* – put her hair in curlers. She'd send Norma to the PMU, the French equivalent of the British Tote betting shop. Norma would join the queue to place bets on the horses.

Though our mother always claimed to be luckless, when it came to gambling my mother's lucky numbers were eight and eleven. (Mine were one, two and nine; the number of my train in my locomotive set. They were never lucky as I don't remember ever winning.) Norma remembers how we waited, and waited, for a whole afternoon in the park as our mother gambled in the nearby casino d'Enghien. Every now and again, Maurice would nip out of the casino to check on us.

By Monday, Maman was just the ticket for Maurice, even if Norma and I had missed out on the attention. She would not get up early on Monday mornings to wish farewell to Norma, who had to fold up the divan chair on which she slept before taking the bus and then the train back to boarding school. (Nor did she say goodbye to me in that short period when I was at boarding school.) And now I find myself thinking about the age-old belief that the children of lovers are orphans.

Maman was sure to be ready for Maurice: always elegantly dressed, classically, and with high-heeled shoes (which Norma would wear from time to time). Her hair was perfect, and she wore one of two perfumes, *Arpege de Lanvin* or *Femme de Rochas* (Norma also wore her perfumes sometimes). Our mother introduced me to *Eau Sauvage*, which was Maurice's favourite, and she wore it occasionally. Sixty years later it is still my favourite.

At their Monday rendezvous, Maurice and my mother would have lunch at Brasserie des Gobelins, just around the corner from home, and I'd meet them for dessert. First, I'd go to the *boucherie chevaline* (the butcher specialising in horse meat) and buy a steak haché or some horse liver. I'd cook the liver with burned onions or tinned beans, or would warm up a tin of cassoulet. Afterwards, I'd join Maurice and my mother at the restaurant for a dessert which, usually, was Gervais mystère au chocolat, ice cream and meringue in a chocolate praline case. *Miam, miam.* I'd sit and eat ice cream, as they chatted and laughed in a fog of Lucky Strike cigarette smoke.

My mother's talents in the kitchen were unquestionable. She was an excellent cook. She was great at savoury dishes, was adept at lobster Thermidor, sauté de veau Marengo and filet de veau en sauce. She was a carnivore's dream, and made a superb boeuf bourguignon, rôti de bœuf en cocotte, and filet de boeuf avec sauce. When she ventured vegetarian-wards, it was to make ratatouille, but that was also superb. Norma was admonished if she returned from the market with lettuce: my mother would inspect the leaves and see that the market seller had sold his old produce to the child.

Our mother was not a desserts person. Patisserie was not her thing. The few sweet dishes that she cooked were limited to gâteau de riz with caramel sauce, and crème caramel, which was my favourite. On Sunday evenings, our mother would hand some francs to Norma and me, and send us to a charcuterie in Avenue des Gobelins, under instructions to buy *des quasis* (pork meat attached to the bones, and excellent to pick at with a knife).

Rather than a sweet finish, Maman preferred cheese, as, apparently, did Norma and I. (One day I went to the market and asked the cheese seller for a camembert to be cut in two, as I wanted only half. He cut it in half, and then when I saw the inside was perfectly ripe, I asked for the whole camembert.) Norma, I think, got rather fed up with the incessant focus on food, but I was a young connoisseur. I cannot claim to have learnt to cook at my mother's knee; we did not cook together. But I cooked as a child, and still enjoy cooking but don't do enough of it. Apart from my horse steak haché, back then I mastered *veau avec oignons braisés* (veal with braised onions). I'd make spaghetti with tomato sauce and caramelised onions, topped with lots of cheese and then finished in a hot oven. I cooked steak au poivre, and not to mention – but I shall – soufflé au Grand Marnier.

The problem with my mother's cooking was that at the table it was necessary to fully appreciate the food, and to be told – by her – exactly how the dish had been made. Then there was the experience of eating out with Maman, again a painful experience. The food was never as good as she would have made it; the chef was always regarded as an inferior being.

Eleven

The Vanishing Au Pair

'Norma, will you come to my office, please?' My half-sister followed the headmistress to her office, unsure of the reason for being summoned. Had she been naughty? Had she been insolent to a teacher? In the headmistress's office there was a blond-haired man sitting in a chair at the front of the desk.

'Norma,' said the headmistress, waving a hand towards the stranger by way of introduction, and the man stood. '*Bonjour Norma*,' he said. '*Je suis ton père*.' That was how Norma met her father. She was thirteen or fourteen years old. She remembers that her body began to shake with nervousness, anxiety, confusion. She could not find the words to respond. She would later tell me, 'I was thinking, what is all this about? What on earth is happening?'

It was shortly afterwards, in 1956, that he came to see Norma. I have no recollection of his visit, other than the memory of a photograph being taken of Norma and me sitting on his motorbike. Then that was it. Either Jean decided not to pursue the relationship, or maybe Norma did not want to stay in touch with her father.

Alternatively, my mother intercepted, and helped to break the bond.

Whatever the case, Jean disappeared from our lives, and from France, and returned to Cambodia. Then, and this must have been in the early 1960s, we were in the South of France. My mother was having another operation. We were supposed to be on holiday, but holidays for us were really a series of operations and illnesses. Anyway, we were in the South of France, and the three of us were sitting outside on a terrace. 'Norma, I just want to tell you something,' began my mother. 'I received a letter. Your father is dead, so now you can only count on me.' And that was how Norma learned of her father's death. Her father the pharmacist, so the story went, had died from an overdose. Not only did Jean give drugs, he also took them.

News of Jean's death was delivered in typical Maman-fashion. Some might say the words came out of her mouth in a particularly harsh way. But she really was capable of launching weapons of mass destruction without realising what she had done. For instance, she had explained to Norma and me, 'You should be grateful that you both escaped the bidet.'

Much later on, when Norma tried to get closer to my mother at some stage, they were in Dinard, on the beach, and our mother was about seventy-five, but with no signs of dementia. She said to Norma, 'I don't understand why you never had children.'

'I didn't want a child to be brought up with a single mother,' said Norma. 'And Gerald's age difference was a problem and he did not particularly like children.'

Marcelle said, 'Children are very useful.' Now, what she meant precisely may have been what she actually said. However, Norma (and I, for that matter) would interpret it like this: children had indeed been very useful to our mother, when it came to her relationships with the commandant, with Raoul, and with Maurice. She was able to present herself as a vulnerable woman who needed help. She said this not in a nasty way, but as if she was delivering wise advice.

At the age of seventeen, Norma had left school and didn't quite know what to do with her life. This is where Danièle, my mother's step-daughter, became very useful. Shortly before he died, you'll recall, my father had begged my mother and Danièle to heal their rift. Now, they were never to become the closest of friends but, as I have said, they certainly tried to get along. And Danièle said, 'I've got a girlfriend in London. She has two children, and she is looking for an au pair.'

The timing was perfect, as my mother was probably wondering what to do with Norma. The opportunity for Norma to learn English (as well as having one of her children out of the way) was not to be missed. 'Norma, London!' So Norma, at the age of eighteen, went to London. Her new boss, the mother of the two children, was wealthy. Her husband, Michael, was twenty-nine. He was a few years younger than his wife, and eleven years Norma's senior.

Well, Norma was an au pair until, that is, the middle of one night – I remember it well – when the phone rang in our apartment. It was Norma's boss, the mother of the two young children, calling from London. 'Marcelle,' she said, 'I have found Michael in Norma's bed without his pyjamas.' Michael was thrown out of the marital home, understandably, and off he went, but with the teenage au pair, my favourite half-sister, Norma. They set up home in a rented flat at 11, Netherton Grove, off the Fulham Road, close to Chelsea and Westminster Hospital.

*

Perhaps it is time to introduce the Sri Lankan-born Dr Emil Savundra. He was a black marketeer, a swindler and a fraudster who, by then in his early sixties, had worked his way around the world, although really there wasn't much work involved. Savundra was a conman extraordinaire, but masterful at conning partly because he was intelligent and well-spoken. He was posh and well-read which, interestingly, made him a plausible businessman. (Today, we are more relaxed about a person's background – sometimes the humbler the roots, the better.)

Savundra's girlfriend, Mandy Rice-Davies – she gained notoriety through the Profumo scandal – would later describe him as a larger-than-life character. 'Well-born Ceylonese, with a brilliant mind he could have made his fortune in any number of legitimate businesses,' she said, 'but chose instead to give his life that added zest by looking for the dishonest twist in everything he did.'

Anyhow, Savundra had settled in Britain and acquired at least two large houses: one in Old Windsor, Berkshire; another in Hampstead. Being a crook, he knew that he required a crooked lawyer. Put simply, Michael was that lawyer.

In 1963 Savundra formed the Fire, Auto and Marine Insurance Company (FAM), a scam that took advantage of the thriving motor insurance industry when car ownership in the UK was increasing and road networks were being developed. Essentially, FAM'S customers – working men and women – paid a premium and Savundra put the money into his own private account, somewhere offshore. Claims, meanwhile, were not paid. Eventually – in 1968 – he would be convicted for the fraud and imprisoned. Before his arrest, the Board of Trade had demanded to see the company's books, and Savundra fooled them by producing a fake document from Liechtenstein. The document stated that FAM had more than £500,000 in government bonds.

Which takes us to Michael, now Norma's lover. He had compiled the forged document from Liechtenstein, but everything, as always, was a big secret.

I was in my early teens when I went to London to stay with

Norma and Michael. It was just a short holiday, and at the end of it the three of us would travel to Berck in France. There, we would spend the weekend with our mother, as well as Renée and Joseph who came from Berck (they left Paris and fled there, you'll recall, with Henriette and Danièle at the outbreak of the war).

We would drive in Michael's smart Citroën DS19, from London to Lydd airport in Kent. Then we'd put the car on the plane and fly with it, on the short flight to Le Touquet. From there, we'd make the thirty-minute drive to Berck. That was the plan. This is what happened.

On the day of travel, Michael, Norma and I carried our suitcases, as well as Michael's briefcase, from the flat and down to the car that was parked outside. Then we drove off to the airport. On the way, Michael asked me, 'Patrice, did you pack my briefcase in the car?'

'Erm. No, Michael. I did not pack your briefcase.' Call me stupid, but I had not considered his briefcase to be my responsibility. Michael went into a rage. 'You are so stupid, Pat,' he yelled. He did a U-turn, and we drove back to where we had started, back to the pavement outside the flat. No briefcase. There was, however, a note on the front door. It read: 'Briefcase on the pavement handed over to the police.' England prides itself on lost and found organisational skills. Norma and I thought that was excellent news. Problem solved.

'Well, at least the police have it,' I said. And Norma nodded. 'Phew, thank God for that.' We shared a sense of relief.

But Michael's face had turned ashen. He said nothing as we drove to the police station, and spoke only when he got out of the car, as he barked an instruction to Norma and me: 'Don't move. Wait here.' We watched as he walked into the police station. A few minutes later he reappeared, carrying the briefcase. He was smiling. The crisis was over, and we made our way to France. Later we discovered that the briefcase had contained incriminating documents detailing Savundra's plan. Had the police found them,

Michael could have ended up in jail… earlier than he did. Whether it was a plan set up by Savundra, or Michael's solution to the fraud, remains a mystery.

After the weekend in Berck, I returned to Paris with my mother, while Norma and Michael went back to London.

Then things began to turn messy for Emil Savundra. He fled to Switzerland and then to what was then Ceylon (now Sri Lanka). Shortly afterwards, in the summer of 1966, FAM was wound up, leaving 400,000 motorists unprotected.

Michael also had to leave London. With Norma, he went to Geneva. Next, they went to Israel, or was it Majorca? I can't recall, but mostly they went to any country that did not have an extradition treaty with Britain. They lived luxuriously, indulging themselves in one five-star hotel after another, though never staying long enough to risk being captured and questioned.

To pay for their lifestyle, Michael, I believe, received hush money from Savundra. My mother and I, on the other hand, received postcards from Norma and Michael. On one occasion, my mother and I flew to Geneva to see Norma, and she told us, 'We're changing hotels regularly as Michael is waiting for some big deals to come through.' Then, shortly after that visit, there was silence. A month passed, and then another, and still no word from Norma. Michael was so good at hiding that we were unable to seek. Norma had gone. To where, we did not know.

Our mother, meanwhile, had endured more chronic dismantling of her strangely chaotic existence.

Twelve

The Lover Leaves

Maurice could never marry my mother. He could never become step-father to Norma and me. As we know, he had told my mother that, because he was a Catholic, he would never divorce his wife. Such is the dichotomy of religion: adultery is possible, divorce is impossible. Even if he had divorced his wife, he would never have been able to marry my mother in a Catholic church. To the day of her death almost, Marcelle maintained – quite rightly, too – that she could still marry in church as she had never married in church.

So Maurice and Marcelle could not exchange vows and rings at the altar, but they had exchanged rings nevertheless. As a symbol of their love, Maurice and Marcelle each wore a ring that was identical; his and her rings.

Did Maurice's wife know of the affair? We will never know for sure, but my mother told me of an encounter she'd had with Maurice's wife in Boulevard Montparnasse. 'I was with Maurice and we were walking, close to his home,' said Maman. 'Suddenly he saw his wife. I had never seen her before. Maurice saw his wife and his wife saw him. He had to introduce us. Of course, he did. He said to her, *"Je te présente Madame Saiman, ma cliente..."* And his wife and I smiled at each other and shook hands. And as we did so, she looked down at my hand and – I am sure of it – she saw the ring. She saw that I was wearing a ring that was identical to Maurice's ring.'

I was happy when Maurice was there because my mother was happy. He put her in a good mood and mostly if she was happy then I was happy. Maurice and I could talk about football and sport. Sure, in those early days my mother had kept their relationship a secret, but once I got to know him, I liked him and, though he was a nice guy, he could not replace my father.

There was an episode when – and for whatever reason – I shouted back at Maurice, 'You cannot tell me what to do. You are not my father.' This must have hurt him because we didn't talk to each other for a few days after that. One day, however, I was walking with my mother and Maurice, I put my hand in his hand and the matter was settled, the rift was healed. I am not sure whether I was right or wrong to shout back, but I feel that as an adult it should not be the role of the child to try to make up.

It was a Thursday afternoon in March 1962, and I was thirteen years old, when I came home from school and, as I put the key in the front door, I heard the hysterical sobs – the uncontrollable breathless wailing – of my mother. *'Il... est... mort, Patrice. Maurice est mort...'*

Maurice's death was not sudden, not unsurprising. In the previous year he had been diagnosed with cancer of the stomach. He had begun to slip, to go downhill. The cancer spread to his liver and from there... Well, it was probably just a question of time. My mother had visited him in hospital. His secretary, the go-between, would tip off my mother, letting her know times it was safe for her to visit, as Maurice's wife would not be at his bedside. What a strange scene it must have been for the doctors and nurses to observe: the sorrowful wife departs; the distraught mistress arrives shortly afterwards.

Maurice had died nine years to the month after the death of Raoul. Both men were in their early fifties when they died. Nine years after losing the father I had never really known, I had now lost the man who I did know could never be my step-father.

And then, decades later, I would try to consider, to reflect upon its effect on my mother. I would try to do this with the help of Anne-Marie, the analyst and the woman who became like my mother. 'You see,' said Anne-Marie, during one of our therapy sessions, 'imagine a scenario… imagine that your mother had no legs. She would be unlike your friends' mothers. Now, you'd be angry that she couldn't walk like the other mothers. But you couldn't blame her.' That's true. I had to agree with Anne-Marie, and I nodded. She added, 'Your mother was mentally crippled. For instance, when she lost her husband, she was left alone in her world. She was not able to leave that world and to think, for instance, of the four-year-old boy – her son – who had lost his father.' Anne-Marie was right. I could also almost hear my mother's voice in my head, saying, '*Je suis une veuve avec deux enfants à charge. Ce n'est pas le moment de me déranger.*' I am a widow with two children to look after. This is not the time to bother me.

Aren't we all impaired in some way? The questions are: how do we deal with our frailties and disabilities, and are we able to do so? Are we able to make the most of what we have? Can we see an opportunity to learn? A lot of questions, but no easy answers, unfortunately. Thinking about it, my mother did find opportunities during her whole life, and she survived. So there may be a lesson there but, of course, she created a lot of ripples but with no idea she'd created them.

She was always being *left alone*. When the Nazi commandant had returned to Germany at the end of the war, Marcelle was left alone. When her husband Jean had caught a plane to begin a new life in Cambodia, Marcelle was left alone. When my father, Raoul, freshly shaved and ready for a holiday in Juan-les-Pins, had suddenly succumbed to that fatal lumbar puncture, she was again left alone. And now, with the death of Maurice, Marcelle was left alone once more. My mother was not a nasty person. It was more that she had problems when it came to thinking of others, and she felt that so often she had been abandoned. She was right.

Only four months away from her fortieth birthday, she was in a position now to look back, take stock and conclude that her life was one long, miserable tale of tragedy and wretched ill fortune. Then, and for years to come, she would say, 'Why am I so unlucky? Why do I never have any good luck? Nothing lucky has ever happened to me.' Perhaps her bleak, mantra-like insistence had an effect upon me – it made me the opposite. When a bad thing happens to me, I tend to think that something good will come of it or, at the very least, may come of it.

For many years I maintained that my father's death at a young age provided me with an opportunity to idealise him. He was absent, he was gone, and this enabled me to make him what I wanted him to be. His death, of course, had stripped him of the opportunity to show me that he was not as good as I saw him to be. Whereas my mother had almost authorised me to be free, to do whatever I wanted. When I became a father, I would try to be the best, and to this day that is still what I try to do, determined to protect my children in the ways I was not protected.

When I began those sessions with Anne-Marie, she guided me to see (at a somewhat late stage) that I had painted my own distorted picture of my father. The picture had helped me tremendously in my adult life, but maybe it was now time to revisit the reality known to that little boy, who lost his father at the age of four. 'And let's start the work,' she said. That was the toughest thing I ever had to do in my life.

Maurice's funeral took place in a Catholic church in Paris. I did not go. Instead I spent the day with my friend, Claude, playing football. At the front of the church, Maurice's wife – no, his *widow* – sat just a few feet from the priest as he conducted the service. Right at the back of the church, sat my mother – mistress of Maurice. She was there alone, perhaps looking down as she played with the eternity ring on her finger, thinking about those nine years with the man she would call 'the love of my life'. And then she left.

For the rest of her life, she kept a large framed photograph of Maurice, arms crossed and in his judo gear, on the wall of her bedroom, alongside a portrait photograph of herself, taken around the same time. So Marcelle and Maurice had been parted, but still, they were always together.

A day or two after the funeral, Marcelle spoke to Maurice's secretary, the go-between. That is when my mother learned that mourners at the funeral had been asking, 'Where are Maurice's wife and his children? Why aren't they here?' Those asking the questions were Maurice's colleagues, the ones who had seen us every Thursday, when we ate lunch together in the basement brasserie of Le Palais de Justice. Mistakenly, of course, they believed that my mother was Maurice's wife. And they believed that Maurice was my father, which was precisely what I wanted my school friends to think.

My mother always saw herself as the one who had been left. At times though she was the one who did the leaving. She left home at the age of sixteen or seventeen because, she always said, she was sick of cleaning and caring for her younger sisters, Thérèse and Michele. Even back then, there were the early signs that she was not a natural carer. I have mentioned Michele, who did in fact care for Norma when the latter was sent there as a small child. Michele read to Norma at bedtimes and seemed a kind-hearted aunt.

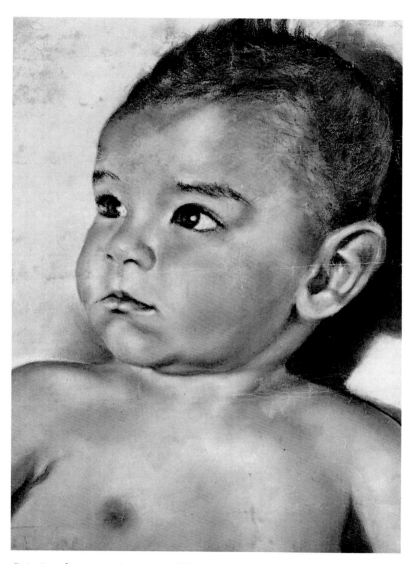

Painting from a prison, 1950. This one-metre square water colour was painted by a client of my father. My father provided him with a photograph of me, and the client painted this while in prison. On the back of the painting, he wrote a poem about that little boy's future – a bright future written by someone whose own future was uncertain. Unfortunately, the painting was restored and during the process its back was covered by cardboard. So the poem remains a secret... except in my mind.

I

Family home: 2, Square la Bruyère. Our apartment was on the fourth floor.

My father, Norma and me, in front of Albert's deli, rue de Rosiers, 1950.

My father and me, 1950.

My father, Norma and me, Parc Monceau, 1952. It was here that I lost le ballon rouge.

Norma and her father, Jean Philippon, 1952.

Danièle, aged four, looking happy in the snow.

Patricia, also at the age of four, with her grandparents.

Here I am, two years old, and with my father in rue des Rosiers.

My mother in 1945.

My mother, 1962.

My father's war medals: Legion d'Honneur; the Cross of the Liberation of Paris; Croix de Guerre; Medaille des Evades; Bataille de Sedan; 2nd Division Blindée (led by Marechal Leclerc).

The Egyptian Prince. It was aboard this steamship that the only listed passenger, Raoul Saiman, arrived in Cardiff on 3rd October, 1942. Just one of his many adventures, and he was on his way to meet General de Gaulle.

With Norma, Beirut, 1958.

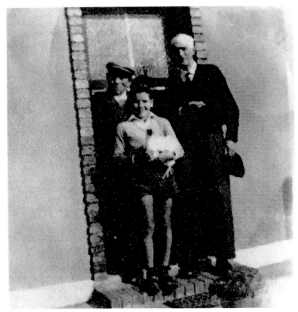

Joseph, Camille and me. Oh, and Oscar my pet cockerel.

Parti « Autour
du Monde » à la
chasse aux talents,
un producteur li-
banais découvre à
Vienne ce petit
camelot pétillant
d'intelligence et
cette jeune Autri-
chienne habillée
de valse et de
gaîté. Il n'en feut
pas plus à l'imagi-
⋯⋯ ⋯⋯ ⋯⋯
transporter à tra-
vers l'espace et le
temps, jusqu'à l'é-
poque brillante
conservée intacte
par la baguette
magique de Jo-
hann Strauss. (Voir
p. 16)

Samedi 30 Juin 1962, 3ème Année — No. 136 — 60 P.L.

IX

Beirut, and learning my lines for a TV play.

My only photograph in uniform. Outside Norma's flat in Boulogne, March, 1970.

La Bonne Auberge, Ile d'Oléron, 1972.

Norma leaves Michael's trial at the Old Bailey in London, July 1964.

Norma, Michael and my mother in Geneva, June 1962.

On my father's grave, 2015.

Anne-Marie Sandler

Leading psychoanalyst who worked with Anna Freud

Anne-Marie Sandler found the work of Sigmund Freud compelling, but after a strict and traditional upbringing she read his work in secret and with a sense of great shame.

When she started studying psychology her tutor "allowed me to feel as though I hadn't been a naughty girl", and that Freud's work was not "all very dirty because it was all about sex. Now very respectable people were saying that Freud was a genius."

As she established herself as one of Britain's leading child psychoanalysts, Sandler worked for several years in London with Freud's youngest daughter, Anna, who is widely regarded as the founder of child psychology. On first meeting Sandler at the Hampstead Clinic in 1950, Anna produced her own version of a "Freudian slip" by asking what undergarments Sandler was wearing. "She said, 'Are you wearing warm underwear? It is very important here with all the draughts and dampness of English houses.'"

During these years Anna Freud arranged for Sandler to work part-time at a nursery school for the blind, where she could watch the behaviour of

Anne-Marie Sandler worked to the age of 90. Below: as a child

20th century because of rising antisemitism. Her father, Otto, was an intellectual who managed a department store; while her mother, Hildegard (née Oberdorf) was a French teacher.

Anna-Marie spent much of her early life with a German nanny whom she called Fräulein. Everything changed in 1933. "My father explained that a very bad man called Hitler had become the leader of Germany. He was bad because he was 'a terrible bully', particularly persecuting Jewish people, but that

fashioned Teutonic manners — she was brought up to curtsey to guests — went down well with Freud, who liked formality.

At about this time she met Joseph Sandler, a Jewish psychoanalyst from South Africa who became a leading theoretician of the Freudian school. After the death of his first wife, Hannah, from cancer, he asked Anne-Marie whether she would babysit for his daughter. She was already charmed by his self-deprecating humour. They married in 1957 and collaborated on many books and papers.

They had two children: a daughter, Catherine, who runs an executive coaching practice; and a son, Paul, who is managing director of an independent TV production company. Her stepdaughter, Trudy McGuinness, is a psychoanalyst. Joseph died in 1998.

Sandler later trained as an adult psychoanalyst at the British Psychoanalytical Society and started her own practice. She was active in several professional bodies, and organised an annual meeting of British and French psychoanalysts. In 1998 she received the Sigourney Award for outstanding achievement in psychoanalysis.

The Times *obituary of Anne-Marie, August, 2013.*

Liz and me, the very happy couple. On our wedding day at The Savoy hotel, 24th January, 1976.

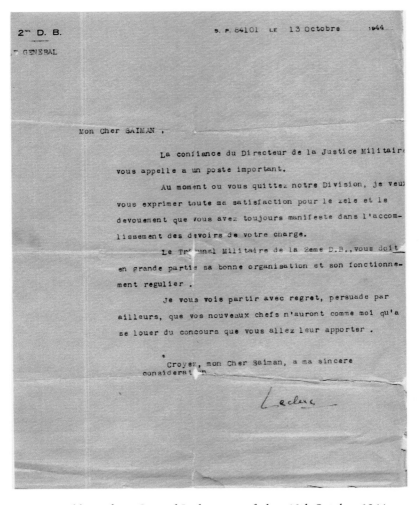

Mon Cher SAIMAN,

La confiance du Directeur de la Justice Militaire vous appelle a un poste important.

Au moment ou vous quittez notre Division, je veux vous exprimer toute ma satisfaction pour le zele et le devouement que vous avez toujours manifeste dans l'accomplissement des devoirs de votre charge.

Le Tribunal Militaire de la 2eme D.B., vous doit en grande partie sa bonne organisation et son fonctionnement regulier.

Je vous vois partir avec regret, persuade par ailleurs, que vos nouveaux chefs n'auront comme moi qu'a se louer du concours que vous allez leur apporter.

Croyez, mon Cher Saiman, a ma sincere consideration

Leclerc

Personal letter from General Leclerc to my father, 13th October, 1944.
Leclerc thanks my father for his service to the famous 2e Division Blindée
(Second Armoured Division), the first division to arrive in Paris when the
city was liberated.

Michelle and her husband, José, who was a military man, lived in Germany, in Friedrichshafen beside the shores of Lake Constance. One summer Norma was due to spend her school holidays with them. José drove to Paris to collect Norma. With her characteristic guile, my mother said to him, 'Will you take Patrice, as well, please?' He nodded. So I packed and left with Norma, which meant my mother could devote more time to Maurice.

After an eight-hour drive to Friedrichshafen, we walked into the house and I saw Michelle standing at the top of the staircase. And she saw me but was not happy. 'What are you doing here?' she said from the highest step. I must say, I've had warmer welcomes. José possibly felt that he'd been a victim of my mother's artfulness, and he was just as inhospitable as Michelle. When I was licking my lips, he told me not to do so and, 'If you do it again, I'll slap you.' I did and he did. We were to stay with them for a month. Norma protected me from most of the hostility, though nothing could prevent José taking us fishing at four in the morning. It was a ghastly ritual and to this day I still hate the idea of putting worms on a hook.

But what of Thérèse, our other aunt? Like my mother, Thérèse had also wanted to leave the family home at the earliest opportunity. She was, like my mother, desperate to get away from her parents. And quite far away, at that. She met Marcel Tamraz by correspondence organised through a dating agency, as was often the way in those days. Hooked up via an agency, one person would write to another, and then the other would write back until sufficient letters established that they were a suitable enough match to meet. Anyhow, that is how Thérèse and Marcel came to meet, and they became more than just good pen friends. Marcel was a fair bit older than Thérèse, and he was Lebanese.

They met for the first time in Paris, and he said something along the lines of, 'Will you marry me?' And then, 'Will you come and live in Lebanon?' Yes to both questions. She had wanted to leave home and was probably happy to leave France. Marcel's personality and looks were probably not the objective, but he was from a wealthy family background, and in Beirut he had a successful business. I am not entirely sure how long Thérèse and Marcel were married but, after she gave birth to their first child, Carol, she embarked on an affair and fell pregnant again.

Putting this into context, most of us have no idea what it is like to survive a war, never mind a world war. Many of those men and women who survived a war must think, 'We've survived! Screw it! Let's do it!' And they have a promiscuous lifestyle. My mother was a survivor, and Thérèse was also a character of considerable grit. While my mother was the single woman attracted to men who were married, Thérèse was the married woman attracted to unattached men.

She had a child, Alain, by her lover. However, she never told Marcel that he was not the father of her new-born son. Quite how she managed to pull that off remains a mystery because Marcel was dark-haired and dark-skinned, but Thérèse produced a son who was fair-skinned and blond. No matter. Marcel may have wondered, what difference would it make? Theirs was a marriage of convenience: Marcel had a wife who was much younger than him, and he had two children; Thérèse, meanwhile, had a comfortable lifestyle.

Which she left temporarily in March 1962 after she received a phone call from my distraught mother. '*Thérèse, il est mort... Maurice est mort.*' Whether Thérèse came to comfort her sister in her moment of need, or whether she came to escape Marcel, I cannot say. But shortly after Maurice's death, Thérèse did leave the Lebanon and she came to Paris with her blond baby, and they stayed with us for a couple of weeks.

One day, a month after Maurice's death, my mother the survivor, announced that she had a plan.

'You are going to the Lebanon,' my mother told me. That was it. I left my school in Paris, Lycée Henri IV, and we flew to Beirut.

Thirteen

Stardom in the Lebanon

A unt Thérèse booked me in to the French school in Beirut, but I would have to wait for the autumn term to begin, and the prospect of doing homework did not appeal to me. However, there were other activities to keep me pretty busy. Namely, acting. Strangely, when my mother had told me I was going to Lebanon, she could have added, 'Where you will become a young star.' You see, I was about to become a young star in the Lebanon.

This came about because Thérèse knew a famous comic actor, René Helou. He appeared on Lebanese television, in a hugely popular weekly show, *Yvette Recoit*. It was a comedy about a family, and starred the nationally adored actress, Yvette Sursock. Every Tuesday, the Lebanese would gather around their TV sets and have a good old laugh. René saw an opportunity to introduce me into the series. 'We could say to the viewers, "This is Patrice. He comes from Paris and he enjoys being with the whole family." We must include Patrice, the viewers would love him.'

And I loved it. I joined the rehearsals, where I'd read my lines, preparing for the thirty-minute shows which went out live. René would collect me from my aunt's apartment, which was only a five-minute walk from the studio. Usually he'd had a couple of whiskies by the time he reached me. René was a heavy drinker and required a few sharpeners before going on stage. After the live show, René would then walk me home. Aunty Thérèse, who would have watched the programme, was full of praise. 'Well done Patrice! You were great! What a star you are!' She may have gone a bit over the top with the adulation, but I never told her to curb it. How ironic that I was in a show about a family.

René was also producing another programme, which went out every Saturday, and was a talent show for young singers. He wanted the programme to be presented by two young people, an American girl and a French boy. I don't recall my American co-presenter's name, but we were taken to the beach and, sipping fruit juice, we posed for photographs – they were public relations shots to promote us as the new presenters. All went well, I think, although on the first show I saw the man behind the camera making signs at me. I took them to mean we had to close the show. In fact, he was making signs to tell me there were five minutes left. The result is that there was a hopeful guitarist who was expected to sing but who ended up being extremely cheesed off. I felt awful at the time, but René, whisky tumbler in hand, said, 'Don't worry, Patrice. You did a fantastic job.'

Then I landed a part in a play which was set in Austria, and told the story of a local singer – my sister – who was involved with a bad guy, and I was there to save her. I was not yet fourteen, and whisked up in the exciting whirlwind of showbiz. My performance in the play led to more PR – I appeared on the front cover of a TV magazine. René said that I was the first Jew to achieve this (and I felt Jewish), and yes, of course, I kept the magazine's front cover as a memento. Within weeks of arriving in Beirut, an extraordinary thing was happening: I was on my way to becoming a household name (in Lebanese households).

As a result of this success, I was called by a producer from another channel. He offered me a part on Channel 9, a competitor of Tele Orient. I did not check with anyone (I was only fourteen, after all) and said that I would be delighted to accept. Thérèse asked me about the phone call and I relayed the conversation. She phoned René who was furious, and made it clear that I would not take the part. He did not want me to appear on a rival station.

My aunty's affair with the father of her blond baby required trips to the beach. There, she would disappear with her lover, while I stayed on the beach, waiting for her to reappear an hour or so later. One afternoon I was lying on the sand reading a magazine, when suddenly some youngsters came up to me and handed me a piece of paper and a pen. They seemed to want my name and address. Strange, I thought, but I wrote my name and address – ensuring the words were legible. The youngsters said, 'Thank you.' They were happy and off they went. My aunt came back, also happy, and in the car on the way home I told her what had happened. 'They wanted your autograph,' she said, and laughed. That was the only time I have been asked for my autograph, even though I did not know I was being asked for an autograph. I was content. My life had purpose and ambition, and my career was certain: I would become an actor.

*

I'd savoured my first taste of notoriety some years earlier. In 1956, when I was at primary school in rue de l'Arbalète, Danièle introduced my mother – and seven-year-old me – to a film producer, Guy Jorré. His production company, Tadié Cinema, was making a commercial for Evian and I landed a role because I was considered to be really cute. The other thing is, Guy and Danièle were very close.

The shoot lasted a week. Maman told the school, 'I'm sorry, but

Patrice is unwell so won't be at school for a while.' During the day there were rehearsals for a couple of hours, filming in the afternoon and then at six in the evening we'd go downstairs to a cinema room to watch the "rushes" (the footage from that day), and that's when Guy and co would decide what to edit. That was the first time I saw myself on a big screen, and it was cool.

There was, however, one episode which left me in tears. During the rehearsal Guy said to me, 'Don't look at the camera. The camera captures your every eye movement. If you look at the camera, we'll need to cut the sequence. It's a big headache.' I nodded like I could obey, but I couldn't. Of course I kept looking at the camera, and Guy was not pleased. Eventually, I managed to do the scene without looking at the camera and, come six o'clock and the rushes, I could see that Guy was right: the slightest glance at the camera appeared giant on the big screen.

The commercial was screened in cinemas, although after giving a week of my life to make it, I never did see the finished product. Ecole de l'Arbalète was split into a school for boys and another for girls, and the commercial was shown at the girls' school. Some of the girls waited for me at the school gates when the final bell rang. They wanted to tell me that they had seen me on screen. This group included two girls who lived in the same block of flats as me, and I was suitably smug and delighted. Appearing in that commercial was an act of one-upmanship that propelled me way above my classmates.

The following year, at the grand age of eight, I won a football competition and the prize was an appearance on a TV programme that was broadcast on Sundays, and presented by Raymond Marcillac, then a well-known sports personality. So there I was, on TV on a Sunday afternoon, and the guest star was Johnny Hallyday, legend of French entertainment. I sat on Johnny's knee, and he asked me about school and questions about football. I brimmed with pride, especially as my schoolmates would be watching and they'd be envious as hell. Some years later, in 1962, and at the age of thirteen, I bought my first record. It was Johnny Hallyday's version of *Da Doo Ron Ron* (or, to give it the correct French title, *Da Dou Ron Ron*).

Fourteen

Escape

In the Lebanon, the fun, the fame, the attention and the job lasted just a few months. I had arrived in Beirut in April, believing we had "emigrated" from France. Then, in August, my mother turned up, having come from Geneva. With her arrival, my new life, which had seemed so extraordinary, suddenly seemed to return to normal, which by anyone else's standards was probably extraordinary.

My mother had been with us for two or three weeks before complaining that she felt ill. Which either meant she was genuinely ill, or it was code which meant: I am not happy in this environment, and so all of us shall have to leave.

Thérèse, by now, had decided that she wanted a divorce from Marcel. With my mother as co-conspirator, she had cooked up a plan to take her to freedom. Thérèse would leave the marital home and come with us, first by passenger ship to Marseilles and then by train north to Paris. She would bring the blond child with her. This plan was to be kept secret – if Marcel discovered her intentions, he might try to keep the baby, Alain, that was not his. In Lebanon it was forbidden for women to leave the country with children unless they had the father's permission (even if Marcel was not the father).

My mother and aunt were so adept at keeping secrets that I didn't have a clue, until the morning of the escape. Marcel said au revoir, as usual, as he left the house and went to work. The moment the door closed my mother said, 'Right! Patrice, pack! We've got to catch a boat back to France. Quick, quick, get a move on.' Getting from A to B is easy for lots of people but was by no means a straightforward exercise for my mother and aunt.

Months earlier my aunt had come to us in Paris to comfort my mother and she had then taken me back to Beirut. Now my mother had come to us in Beirut and we were taking my aunt back to Paris.

The escape would involve a cruise, which seemed exciting, but what about my acting? What about my career, my ambition? What about my dream? My mother's reaction said it all: 'Oh, forget about that.' The two sisters dashed around the house, packing bags, gathering possessions. Two large taxis arrived at noon, and we jumped in and zoomed to the port. For reasons I never understood, food was left everywhere, the fridge was left open, and the flat was left in a terrible mess.

At passport control, my aunt presented a letter that she had faked. It gave permission for her to take the child abroad, and was seemingly signed by Marcel. The dummy letter worked a treat and soon we were on the ship, although Thérèse was terribly anxious. She feared that Marcel would arrive or alert the police before we set sail in the early evening. The ship, by the way, was appropriately named *Espéria*, as in "hope".

The cruise would take us first to Alexandria, and then to Messine and Naples, before docking in Marseilles. I suffered terrible seasickness between Beirut and Alexandria, but heard an announcement on the loudspeaker, calling for Thérèse to go to the post room: she had received a telegram. It was from Marcel. 'I beg you. Stop. Please come home. Stop. I love you.' That sort of thing.

This was to be the first in a long stream of telegrams from Marcel, in which he pleaded for his wife to come to her senses and return to Beirut. But he would have to live in... *espéria*. Thérèse never replied.

We visited Alexandria, saw Mount Vesuvius burning at night, went to Pompei and, finally, we arrived at the port of Marseilles. From there we drove to Juan-les-Pins, for a week on the coast. My mother secured a last-minute booking at Hôtel Rescali, the family hotel where we'd holiday as a family when my father was alive.

We stayed there for about a week, but my mother and aunt had grown tired of one another, and they frequently argued. It was time to make another move. My mother disappeared one day and returned a few hours later with a second-hand car, a German-made DKW. Then, with the two sisters bickering about this and that, we began the drive back to Paris. Driving from south to north seems such a simple thing to do, doesn't it? However, we'd been on the road for three or four hours, and were half-way to Paris, when the car stuttered to a halt. The vehicle could be driven, but only at a ridiculously slow speed.

'I know what we can do,' said my mother. She then drove, a bit faster than walking pace, to the little ancient town of Perrecy-les-Forges, prettily perched on the banks of the River Oudrache in Burgundy. Who lived here? My mother's uncle, Pierrot Bouillet. He was a mechanic with a garage, so he'd be able to fix the car. And Uncle Pierrot lived with his wife and his mother-in-law, who was the most enormous woman I had ever seen. Pierrot mischievously called her 'La Libellule' – The Dragonfly.

La Libellule came from Alsace, which meant her nationality changed with the German annexing of the region. She was born French and then had become German during World War I. She was French again at the end of World War I, and she was German at the beginning of World War II. Then she was French once more, when the conflict ended. But who cares whether she was French or German? There was no disputing that this big dragonfly was a tremendous cook.

We received the most wonderfully warm welcome, and I stayed at their house while my mother, Thérèse and baby Alain stayed in a hotel across the bridge. Then my mother and Thérèse – with Alain – took the train to Paris, arguing as they went. I was left with my great-uncle the mechanic, his wife and La Libellule, and relished the respite from the turmoil between mother, aunt and the crying blond baby.

I stayed for two or three weeks perhaps. A bit longer, probably, than it took to fix the car. I helped my great-uncle in his garage, and he'd take me to the café where he'd have his aperitif – on the way there and back he'd let me sit on his lap and hold the steering wheel. On the way back, I may have done a better job than him at driving. He taught me how to go-kart (he was president of the local karting club). And he would take me to see his mistress, a charming woman. She happened to be the wife of my great-uncle's friend who had a large factory that made bricks.

I ate superb meals cooked by La Libellule, spent a lot of time playing football, and I met a young lady. I can't remember her name but I kissed her and she then told me, 'You don't know how to kiss.' So she showed me how to kiss. I did not like it and thought it was a joke.

At some stage, my mother – never fussed about leaving me on my own – phoned with news. 'Thérèse has gone back to Beirut.' To be frank, I was relieved.

Baby Alain made it back to Beirut, but he would never make it to adulthood. He got to the age of fifteen or sixteen, when, during the Lebanese Civil War, he was dodging bullets with his friends, but he failed to dodge the particular one that proved to be fatal. By then Thérèse had divorced Marcel and had a new husband, Gaby Khaty, and they had a son, Patrick. In the mid-70s, I was on my way to Cairo and the Suez Canal and took a detour to spend an evening with Thérèse and Gaby, and stayed at their flat in Beirut. It was a nice evening, and full of memories of Beirut, but the journey from their flat to the airport – in a country which was still in a civil war – was rather tense, and I was relieved to be on the plane to Cairo.

But back to my mother, phoning with news; 'And I have rented a flat in Fresnes,' she said. 'And I have enrolled you in a new school...'

The flat was in a high building close to Fresnes prison, and the school was rough. It was a rough, unpleasant area. Reflecting on it now, I assume that the cash was finally running out. My mother bought me a bicycle to take me to and from school, and it worked better and was faster than the DKW, which was still being mended by Uncle Pierrot in between his unhurried visits to café and mistress.

It was September 1962, and the Algerian war had ended. This saw the return to Paris of what were now known as the Pieds-Noir – the Black-Feet, the people of French and European origin who were born in Algeria during French rule (from 1830 to 1962), the vast majority of whom departed for mainland France as soon as Algeria gained independence, or in subsequent months. They were not popular because their arrival pushed up the rental market.

Meanwhile, I was sun-tanned after my stint in the Lebanon. I had a Jewish name and was proud to tell my friends that my father was born in Algiers, which was foolish of me. I was labelled 'the pied-noir', in a pejorative way. I tried my best to dig myself out of the hole. 'Actually, I've never been to Algeria. I've lived in Paris all my life. I am this brown because I spent about six months in the Lebanon and did TV shows there.' No one was listening, and I became pretty miserable. I wrote letters to René Helou, and to contacts at the TV channel, but like Marcel, Thérèse's husband who fired off the desperate telegrams, I received no replies.

We stayed just a few weeks in Fresnes, and then rented an apartment at 62 Boulevard Saint-Germain and I returned to the Lycée Henri IV, the school that I had left in March. Having missed out on a couple of terms, I was behind with the curriculum. Looking back, it was a period of movement, from one apartment to another, my mother unable to pay the rent. And, as if I had not attended enough schools, I returned to Lycée Henri IV. This was one of the top schools in Paris and only took me back because I had a good track record there. But by then I was way behind the other pupils.

Fifteen

La Bonne Auberge

Norma and I were delivered into this world by two women. One of them was Marcelle, our mother, who gave birth to us. The other woman was Madame Gauthier. She was the midwife, you'll recall, who was there when Norma and I emerged from our mother, five years apart but both in rue Lauriston, in the clinic which during the war was next to the Gestapo's evil headquarters.

These two women met again, around about 1962. Madame Gauthier was no longer a midwife. Her sister had bought a château in the centre of France, and converted it into a children's home. The place specialised in children who wet the bed, a problem which, back in those days, was met with a father's slap. Madame Gauthier, who with her teenage daughter lived on the top floor of the chateau, invited us to stay.

One day my mother told me, 'We are leaving home today.' We packed our essential belongings into two suitcases, walked out of the flat and closed the door behind us. My mother slid the keys under the front door. We carried our suitcases to a car that my mother had rented. We put the suitcases into the car, and off we drove, to the château for bed-wetting children in the centre of France.

We would stay for an indefinite period of time and never did return to that flat in Boulevard Saint-Germain. I had not forgotten to take my football. It was always with me, and once settled in our new home I'd use it for goal practice against the door of a church near the château.

My mother's relationship with Madame Gauthier developed well, and one day the latter said, 'I want to buy a hotel and am wondering if you would like to manage it. We could be partners.' The hotel, with restaurant, was in the beachside resort of La-Brée-les-Bains, on the north-east coast of Île d'Oléron. '*Mais oui,*' and my mother was in. In fact, Madame Gauthier bought the hotel in my mother's name. We moved to Île d'Oléron in September 1963.

The island, in the Atlantic and just off the west coast of France, had long since established itself as a popular holiday destination, and La Brée, as it is more simply known, was a pretty spot for tourists, with a pleasant, sand-duned beach, forests of pine, a fifteenth-century windmill, and – for the keen anglers who visited – a coastline dotted with plenty of fishing boats captained by weather-beaten-faced fishermen who could charge for a day on the waves. It always helps if a French town can boast a connection to literature, and La Brée can do just that. Pierre Loti, the naval officer, adventurer, novelist and all-round French hero, came here for his childhood holidays and, following his death in 1923, he was buried on the island (and in between he wrote about it in at least one of his novels).

Plus, a bridge was being built that would connect the island to the mainland (opened in 1966, it was then the longest bridge in France). This would increase tourism, which would be good for my mother's new business. The hotel was called La Bonne Auberge, and sometimes I would help out as a waiter. My mother was the manager and, from an early stage, she was good at drinking the profits. If a customer invited her for a glass of champagne, she accepted, of course, and then it was: 'Patrice, bring us a bottle of champagne.' This next bottle was on the house.

New place meant new school, of course. I became a pupil at a lycée in Le Château-d'Oléron, half an hour's drive from La Bonne Auberge. I'd go by school bus in the mornings, and most afternoons my mother would pick me up (my Great-Uncle Pierrot had fixed the second-hand DKW, and Maman and I had collected it on our way from Paris to the Gauthier château).

This was a mixed school, with girls and boys, and the equivalent of a British middle school, but with a great deal of volleyball, the island's favourite sport. I'd be a pupil here for two years, until passing the *brevet d'études du premier cycle* (BEPC; the school certificate that was taken at the age of about sixteen). Then I'd go to boarding school in Saintes on the mainland for three years, in order to achieve my *baccalauréat*. Well, there you have it; that was the plan.

My time at the school in Le Château-d'Oléron, and my performance, were both average. I was neither the best pupil, nor the worst, though I had a certain amount of stability in my life. Reflecting on it now, I lived comfortably, very close to the sea in a small village. La Bonne Auberge was only fifty metres from the beach, and my bedroom was in the hotel. At night I was sent to sleep by the splashing of waves. My mother, too, could boast that she had her own small hotel, which was merely the dream of many people. (Admittedly, the hotel had been bought with someone else's money, and I understood that the cash from Madame Gauthier was not entirely legitimate as it came from undeclared income from the children's home. But why should I care?) My mother and I would eat in the kitchen, listening to the radio. Agreed, life was not as exciting, not as buzzy, as our previous existence in Paris, but it was the closest we could get to normality, with days often spent looking forward to the next summer.

Memories of that period are mostly cheerful. I recall barbecues on *sarment de vigne* (vine branches) and mixing with the villagers and fishermen, and volleyball games with the other children of La Brée. Being soccer mad, as you know, I joined the football team of Saint-Pierre-d'Oléron. (We played every Sunday, and I'd make the twenty-minute drive by velo motor.) Claude, my dear friend, was far away in Paris, but I made a few friends at the school. I was closest to André Drossard, the son of a pharmacist in Saint-Pierre-d'Oléron.

*

Summers on the island were busy, as tourism thrived. I had a variety of jobs in our little hotel. I set tables in the dining room and stocked the bar with bottles from the cellar. I shucked oysters, and cleaned the mussels, tugging away their beards, so they were ready for the pot. I got bread from the baker whose boxer dog, Cora, adored us and would follow me back to La Bonne Auberge. She liked me, I think, but she also knew that she'd be fed quite well at the hotel. Cora spent more time at La Bonne Auberge than at her own home, and she guarded the hotel's entrance while sunbathing.

The staff included the chef, René, quite a small, rotund guy who lived in the village. There was a girl from the village who helped out, and I'd serve at the bar and as a waiter. At times I vanished to play volleyball on the beach, and I'd be free by 3pm, so was back on the sand with the crowd. In the evening after dinner, I'd join my friends again on the beach, and we'd sit beside a bonfire, chatting away.

We were a big crowd of boys and girls, listening to music on the jukebox, incessantly talking and laughing. Once a week we'd go to an open-air cinema, taking blankets to keep warm (sometimes the film mattered less than the company). Again, that picture of stability, normality, becomes clearer as I write, as I look back on it. We also had volleyball tournaments, playing under floodlights, and crowds gathered to watch. I was a teenager, surrounded by people my own age and it was a long holiday. What else would one want?

The season, however, came and went too fast. By 25th August, there was the mass exodus of holidaymakers, and houses were being locked up for the winter months. Quite a lonely life was setting in, and it would last for another six to eight months. Through the guidance of René the chef, I learnt how to make soufflé au Grand Marnier, omelette Norvégienne (baked Alaska) and coq au vin.

The hospitality industry is a place of drama, eccentricity and madness, and this was no exception. Take, for instance, the case of John. He was a young Englishman who arrived as a guest but then, two days after checking in, he put on a pitiful face and told my mother, 'I am sorry. I cannot afford to pay the bill.' There's that old joke about having to wash the dishes because the bill was too high. That turned out to be a truism on this occasion. John was sent to the kitchen, where he... washed the dishes.

I am not sure how long he was destined to stay as a washer-up, but he seemed to morph from guest to employee. He was still there, in the kitchen, about a week later when the local police arrived at Reception and asked my mother whether John so-and-so was still staying at the hotel. 'We have a warrant for his arrest,' they said. It seems that John had been a soldier in the British Army and was wanted by the military police in connection with a crime he had allegedly committed. John was clearly not the smartest fugitive – not the sharpest knife on the draining board – and on arrival at La Bonne Auberge he had filled in the registration card. The card, along with the others, were routinely sent to the police station. That is when he was rumbled.

John was arrested and taken to the local police station, where he spent a couple of days and nights in a cell. My mother took food parcels to John, so that he could eat well behind bars. And he did indeed eat well. I remember one meal was a particularly handsome lobster. Then we learned that the British Army's military police had arrived on the island. They had come to pick up John, but that was all too simple a plan for my mother. She suggested to the military police that they spend the night at La Bonne Auberge and leave the next morning. They agreed. After all, you cannot go to Île d'Oléron and not try the seafood; it's exceptional.

So, that night they also ate well, and with John at their table. The other guests were quite excited to see what was happening; the islanders had rarely known such excitement. 'What about a nightclub,' someone suggested. Well, the soldiers thought that was a jolly good idea, and so a crowd of about a dozen – John among them – left the hotel and went dancing, and didn't return until the early hours of the following morning. Then, bleary-eyed, the military police left the island with John. We didn't expect to see him again.

There was another person we had not seen. Norma. My mother and I had heard nothing from her for several years. There had been those postcards from her ages ago, as she flitted from one five-star hotel to another with Michael. The correspondence had long since dried up and I missed her a great deal. My half-sister, my soul-mate, my confidante. There were so many times when I wished for a telephone call from Norma, so that I could hear her voice. Or another postcard or a telegram, or a knock on the door.

Sixteen

Captured

There was A fist-clenched pounding on the door. Bang, bang, bang. The final thud was followed by the shout from a man, 'Police!' A second later – *whoosh!* – the detectives were through the door, and in the room. Action, action.

The drama was unfolding in a dingy hotel in Manhattan one night in the spring of '64. One of the FBI investigators flashed a badge, as he said, 'Michael Alterman, I have a warrant for your arrest. You have the right to remain silent. You have the right to refuse to answer questions. You have the right to an attorney.'

The game was up for this particular attorney. 'Michael Alterman, do you understand your rights?' I'm guessing Michael did.

He had spent two years on the run, with Norma at his side. Within an hour the fugitive and his girlfriend were in a police station. There had been the rise and rise of Michael Alterman. This was the downfall. Soon he would be extradited to Britain, where he would face charges of fraud.

Norma was not to be charged with committing any crimes but, to the American authorities, she was a headache. So within a day or so of the FBI raid she was escorted to a plane and sent back to France. And – after two years of hearing nothing – my mother only knew that Norma was alive and well when she received a short telegram: 'COMING HOME STOP SEE YOU TOMORROW STOP LOVE NORMA' She was gone for so long but came back so quickly. Once at L'Île d'Oléron, she helped out with the running of La Bonne Auberge.

Our mother, meanwhile, embarked on a fresh relationship. *L'Homme Martini* – the Martini Man – was the name Norma and I gave to the man who sold (you may have guessed it) Martini to the restaurants and hotels on the island. Most food and drink suppliers would arrive at La Bonne Auberge, have *un café* or aperitif while pitching to my mother. Then they were off, driving away to pitch to someone else. The Martini Man was distinctly different to the others. Often, he'd show up during that *cinq-à-sept* period that I have previously mentioned: five-to-seven is the conventional time (in France) for affairs, those couple of hours after leaving work and before going home.

For years my mother had been Maurice's *cinq-a-sept* lover. She was accustomed to late-afternoon sex, and now it was the Martini Man who helped her to fill that time in the day. I suppose that for my mother, it was a way of dealing with her fear – that fear she had of being alone. As for the Martini Man, La Bonne Auberge must have seemed particularly *bonne*. I don't know if their romance led to a reduction in the price of Martini, but we always seemed to have enough of the stuff to fill Lake Bourget.

Norma and I would hear Martini Man's low voice at the front door, 'Marcelle, bonjour,' and then we'd see him, bearing the grin of someone who knew his lustful expectation would soon be transformed into reality. The two of them would disappear to my mother's bedroom, *Maman et l'Homme Martini*. Inevitably, the time would come when the bar had to be opened, which meant we'd need the cash box but, oh dear, the box was in our mother's bedroom, on the ground floor and beside the kitchen. The scene replays itself in front of my eyes, as if it is happening now...

Norma and I are outside our mother's room. Norma knocks. '*Maman, Maman... Nous avons besoin de la caisse pour le bar... Maman?*'

And then from the other side we hear my mother's voice, '*Attends, Norma. Attends un moment...*' Norma and I wait a moment. Then the door opens, but only wide enough for my mother's naked arm to fit through the space. In her exquisite hand – a hand sometimes adorned by a ring of topaz or a diamond-encrusted eternity ring – in her hand is the handle of the essential cash box. '*Voilà!*' I take the box. The door closes. The bar opens.

*

Not that there was much cash. Money was so tight. I remember occasions when we'd raid other people's vegetable gardens, helping ourselves to potatoes, tomatoes, cucumbers. Salads were added to the menu.

But I was so happy that Norma was back, and there we were, Maman, Norma and I at La Bonne Auberge during the winter. She told Maman and me about the dramatic end of her days on the run with Michael. I was fascinated by the story.

They had arrived in New York with money, and they settled at the Beaux Arts Hotel which sat on 44th Street, between 1st and 2nd Avenues, and near the United Nations building. Long since gone, the Beaux Arts was built in the late 1920s, and made up of apartments. It was used as a temporary residence by visiting United Nations diplomats, and as a permanent residence by established writers and artists.

*

This is Norma's account of the days leading to the arrest:

We had a large studio with kitchenette. And Naitcha, my beloved poodle, was with us, of course. After three or four months, the money ran out. More money was due but we waited for it to arrive from Geneva. It was coming through a Mr Kapoor, another Indian friend of Savundra.

I got a job with a modelling agency that worked with clothing manufacturers in the 7th Avenue neighbourhood. The manager paid me every weekend, would call me 'Good girl', and send me off to the dress and coat manufacturers. I had some success with shop buyers when I walked in and announced the names of dresses or coats with my French accent. When there were no customers I sometimes looked after the switchboard which had a card system that we threaded in holes as soon as it lit up. I got yelled at by the boss because I often cut him off while he was on the phone.

What I earned allowed us to feed ourselves. As for Michael, he started selling encyclopaedias. Sometimes I went with him, laden with books. And we visited families at mealtimes, the best time. Three weeks before his arrest, Michael sold an encyclopaedia to James T. Farrell, the Irish-American novelist. He's best-known for his trilogy of Studs Lonigan books, and he also lived in the Beaux Arts. We'd hit it off with a session of great whisky shots at his place.

Michael would go to the city library, mainly to borrow records by Bruckner, Bartok, Mahler. I was happy to discover their music. Then, there came a time when we stopped paying for the hotel. So we moved to a dingy hotel in Broadway. We were there for about a week, when one night we were playing a game of rummy, and there was a knock on the door. We opened it and there was Interpol in front of us. All I remember is Michael, in handcuffs, taken away by two police officers.

After a horrible night, they came back for me the next morning. As for Naitcha? I was entitled to a phone call. I called James T. Farrell who came to pick him up. I spent a night in jail, in a dormitory full of women. A terrifying night with screaming stomach cramps. Then an agent came to get me and said, 'We'll put you on trial.'

The judge asks me, 'Do you want to stay in the United States or return to France?'

I say, 'Go back to France, but with my dog. And I want to get the money that the modelling agency owes me.'

That same day, the agents helped me pack the bags in the dingy hotel. They took me to the agency to get my money, I don't know how much, but they took half for themselves. What about my dog? 'We have notified James T. Farrell who will take him to the departure of the flight.'

And that was what happened. I was taken to the plane by the agents. They gave my passport to the pilot, and I see a cage with my Naitcha. Still with my stomach cramps, I was crying on Naitcha's head. When I arrived in France, I made my way to La Bonne Auberge. I also learned that Michael left New York on the same day as me, but for London and Wormwood Scrubs.

*

Norma and I spent time together in Île d'Oléron until Michael appeared at the Old Bailey, Britain's foremost criminal court. Then Norma went to London to witness the trial, and was accompanied by our mother. I stayed in Île d'Oléron, and was looked after by a local family.

Michael's con, the court heard, was straightforward enough. He had used forged share and stock certificates to the value of £250,000 as collateral, as well as a forged power of attorney from a "client", in order to obtain a loan of £100,000 from a firm of city merchant bankers, Knowles and Foster. The certificates, and a power of attorney, were in the name of a man called D.H. Morgan. Michael claimed that this "Morgan" fellow had hoodwinked him. However, when checks were made, no person of that name had shares in either of the two companies, Distillers and Great Universal Stores. D.H. Morgan may as well have been D.H. Lawrence.

He had evaded arrests, said the prosecution, by globe-hopping (with my half-sister) – Geneva, Madrid, Rome, the Canary Isles, Israel, Tel Aviv, Canada and the United States of America. As for the money? Police believed it was banked in Switzerland, and not a penny of it had been repaid. Reporters at the trial wrote of Michael as a 'dapper, man-about-Mayfair, who mixed with international criminals'.

The trial of Michael Alterman ended on the same day that Sir Winston Churchill retired as a Member of Parliament: Tuesday, 28th July, 1964. Compare, if you will, the two scenes playing out on that day, in two grand institutions separated by two miles. In the House of Commons, Sir Alec Douglas-Home, the prime minister, stood before fellow politicians and paid tribute to Churchill, to his 'magnanimity… humanity… a man of the strongest principles'. Meanwhile, in the Old Bailey, Judge Aarvold, the Common Serjeant (the second most senior judge of the Central Criminal Court), addressed the court as Michael Alterman stood before him. 'This was,' said Lord Justice Aarvold, 'a careful, imaginative fraud, cunningly conceived and deliberately carried out.'

The judge sentenced Michael to seven years' imprisonment. As her lover was led away in handcuffs to begin his sentence, Norma wept. She told a reporter from the *Daily Express*, 'I love him. I will wait for him.' Which is fine and understandable, but how long would she wait for him?

Of being on the run, she told the *Daily Express*, 'It was not always happy because we always knew that someday, we might have to face this. At times it hung like a shadow over us.' Michael was still legally married, but Norma told the newspaper, 'If there is a divorce I may even come back and ask the prison governor for permission to marry Michael while he is serving his sentence.'

The *Express* devoted most of page eleven to the story, beneath the headline: 'On-the-run love affair ends.' The article began: 'Glamorous Parisian blonde Norma Philippon left the Old Bailey in tears yesterday with her two-year round-the-world runaway romance finally over.'

Michael began his prison sentence behind the bars of Wormwood Scrubs, the high security prison in London. His fellow inmates included George Blake, the British spy who had been convicted of giving national secrets to the Soviet Union. Norma moved to London, so she could be close to Michael, and she lived with a friend in the English capital.

Next, Michael was sent to HMP Leyhill, a cushy, low security – or "open" – prison about fifteen miles north of Bristol. Norma moved to Bristol, so that she was, again, close to Michael.

Norma had created her own distance from our mother. And she had done so in dramatic style, it has to be said. Not everyone gets to escape the family home by going on the run with a fugitive.

We were in our second summer at La Bonne Auberge when Norma returned from her adventures, and came to stay. The two women – mother and daughter – started to attract more people from the village, as they came to the bar of La Bonne Auberge, and the place became a little livelier.

Norma had featured in the British newspapers as "the glamorous Parisian blonde", and she recounted the whole story to my mother and me. We were both deeply fascinated by the intricacies of Michael's deceit, and tales of their days on the run. However, I do not recall these adventures being discussed outside our circle. We were living in a small village on a small island, and the other islanders may not have approved of, or enjoyed the tale.

Interestingly, every month she received, via telegram transfer, the sum of £50. This, she said, came from 'Uncle E'. She also bought the *Daily Telegraph* every day, doubtless keeping up with the news about Uncle. Then one day she saw the front-page news: 'Emil

Savundra Arrested'. She knew then that the pocket money from Uncle E was coming to an end.

*

I was due to take my BEPC in 1964 in La Rochelle. I needed to pass the exam in order to progress to *le baccalauréat*. I did indeed pass, but there was an incident which was quite upsetting, or maybe challenging, and to this day it remains so. While I liked history, I didn't get on with the teacher, a slim woman with long, curly hair and glasses with dark, thick lenses (those problems with her eyesight must have prevented her from seeing my talent).

I had not revised because the marks for history did not merit a massive amount of work. However, it so happened that I had been very interested in the independence of Italy under Garibaldi and King Victor Emmanuel. This particular part of history I knew by heart and, if asked, could have talked about it for hours.

Guess what? Come the exam, and there it was: 'Elaborate on the independence of Italy...' I answered with confidence, and duly received the highest mark the school had ever known. The headmistress broke the good news to me, and she gave me a prize. However, she also said, '*Il y a de la chance que pour les crapules*.' Chance only favours scoundrels. That was not nice and still, years later, I don't know why she said it. Did she think I was too lippy? Or was it just that I came from Paris? I do not know those answers. If only she could have quoted Louis Pasteur: 'Chance favours the prepared mind'.

With the BEPC certificate sorted, the next three years were to have been spent in a boarding school in Saintes. Every Monday Norma would drive me to Le Château where I'd take a ferry to Marennes, on the mainland, and then a school bus would take me and my fellow pupils to Saintes. Every Friday afternoon, it was back by bus to Marennes, followed by the ferry crossing, and then

Norma or my mother would pick me up and the drive back to La Brée. Norma didn't pass her driving test until later on, but my mother did not feel like getting up at six on Monday mornings to take me to catch the ferry to the mainland. Norma had no problem in getting up early simply to have the chance of driving the car.

As with Villard-de-Lans, that home I'd been shipped to after my father's death, there was a regimental routine to the day at this school. We slept in dormitories, breakfasted in a refectory (the food was pleasant), attended lessons, lunched in the refectory, followed by more lessons. We'd be free at 4.30pm, when we were given *pain au chocolat* or *tartine de beurre avec confiture*. On the playground we could play football or volleyball (I played both), and dinner was followed by an hour's study. Then it was bedtime, sleep, and up the next day for the same thing. On Thursday afternoons we were allowed out, so we'd go to the cinema, or for a drink in a coffee shop, or stay closer to home, playing in the schoolyard. As with the chalet at Villard-de-Lans, I enjoyed the routine. And from what I remember, my school work and reports were encouraging.

The teachers were allowed to smoke at school, and so were the pupils. I never liked smoking, but made sure I carried a packet of Gauloises, the cheapest brand of cigarettes, in my shirt pocket. I went further, buying a pipe and Clan pipe tobacco, with its comforting, honey fragrance. I wasn't a natural – after a few puffs I felt completely out of it. I realised that, in order to show I was an adult, I could simply let the pipe hang from my mouth, never actually smoking it, or even having to fill the pipe's chamber with tobacco. It took me three years, until I was in Bristol, that I felt adult enough to tell people that I did not smoke and didn't like it. I still don't, and it probably stems back to my mother and Maurice smoking in the car or in the apartment (I am thankful to them for having shown me the way to a non-smoking life). Of course I did not know then that I would meet and marry a smoker, who would smoke until our first grandchild was born in 2007. (To anyone who wants to quit: persuade your children to have a child.)

One night there was a power strike. It was after dinner, and during our study time, between, say, 8pm and 9pm. A few of us thought it would be fun to make torches by lighting some old newspaper. The smoke led to the windows being opened and, in turn, the draft led to large flames. These, in turn, burnt our hand and so we dropped the "torches" onto the parquet floor which had recently been varnished. We all stamped our feet to extinguish the flames and then swiftly left the room, the smell of smoke hanging in the air. In the morning, after breakfast, the class boarders were told to assemble in front of the headmaster and our teachers. The headmaster said, 'Who started the fire? I need to know what happened. I want the culprit – or culprits – to be outside my office by the end of break.

'If no one comes, then all of the boarders in the class won't be allowed to return home for four weeks. And they won't be allowed to go out on Thursdays for the next four weeks.'

Short and sweet, it was well calculated: the headmaster allowed the pressure from all the other boys during the break to be rather persuasive. André Drossard and I thought we'd better come clean and tell everyone that we'd go to the headmaster. We did. He made us wait for half an hour outside his office. The ticking off wasn't pleasant, although justified, but we were more concerned about the letter to our parents, explaining our crime and punishment: that we would not be able to return home for four weeks and would not be allowed out on Thursday for the next four weeks. We almost became heroes, though I think the others owed us something as they'd been willing participants. I can't recall my mother's opinion on this criminal activity.

Putting that unfortunate episode to one side, the boarding school schedule undoubtedly created the right environment for study, and while there were boarders and non-boarders, it was generally the boarders who achieved the better results. The *baccalauréat* would take three years. The first year was *2-eme*, the second year was *1-ere*, the third year was *terminal*. My first year at boarding school (which was *2-eme*) was promising, and with good results. In the first term of my second year (*1-ere*), September to December, my results were still good.

What happened next was probably a stupid act of youth, and possibly I have no one else to blame but myself. I told my mother that I no longer wanted to stay at the boarding school and that instead I wanted to go back to Paris. I would have been very strong, I assume, or my mother may well have had other problems such as running the hotel (which was probably running out of cash). Yet I was so determined that she caved in and agreed.

I left the boarding school in December 1965, and started at school in Paris, at the Lycée Charlemagne. I lived in a small room at the top of a hotel, near Maurice's previous office at Hôtel de Béthune-Sully.

I had created distance between myself and Maman. It's true, she could not cope with being alone, but *alone* in the sense of not having a man, a lover. If my mother had a man in her life then she was not alone. I was happy, as I have said, when Maurice was around because he made her happy. He cured solitude. And whenever she had a boyfriend, I was content because she had somebody with her.

I am not sure, however, that the prospect of being without her children filled her with dread. Throughout my childhood – or rather, since my father's death – there had been times when she had distanced herself from me, rightly or wrongly. Now, at sixteen, I was in the position of being able to distance myself from my mother. I felt old enough and independent enough to do so.

I did not recognise it at the time but, on reflection, I can see that in order to survive it was necessary for me to get away. By moving to Paris, I could escape the almost unbearable histrionics that were a fixture of life with Maman. And then there had been episodes of aggression. On one occasion I was asking her for some pocket money when, all of a sudden, she flew into a rage. 'If you ask me once more,' she screamed – she picked up a kitchen knife and waved it at me, as if she was ready to stab me – '*Je vais t'éventrer*,' she said. I am going to gouge you. She didn't do it, as you can tell. Maybe she was at the end of her tether, but I was scared. This was not an acceptable mother-son interaction.

*

Years later, when I sat with my mother-replacement, the therapist Anne-Marie, I would also deliberate over the guilt I had about leaving my mother, and I came to realise that by creating distance between us I discovered freedom. The ultimate, the pinnacle of that sense of freedom, came when my mother died. I was free of the burden of guilt. Today, I am as free as ever, even if my mother is still around; she retains a presence, just as ever.

In many ways Norma suffered more than I did. Or let's put it this way, Norma did not recover as well as I did. I tried to encourage her to see Anne-Marie, the woman who had helped me to find freedom. 'Norma, therapy has helped me so much,' I said. 'Helped me to understand about life, and our mother and how she affected us. Why don't you come along for a session with Anne-Marie?' Norma wouldn't dare go there, and Anne-Marie said to me, 'Be gentle. If she doesn't want to, she doesn't want to.'

Throughout my adult life I was shadowed by the guilt of not seeing my mother often enough. And then, when I did see her, I felt guilty because I had nothing to say. I felt that she didn't know me, and that whatever I said was of absolutely no interest to her at all.

When I was about forty-five, or maybe fifty, I visited Maman at her apartment in Paris. We had supper and, as we ate, I said that business was quite difficult, that I was going through a rough patch. I wanted to share this with her. Maybe I wanted her to be a mother, to be supportive and give my life some of her attention. Instead, she responded dismissively, 'Oh yes, yes, yes.' She glanced over the table, and dishes on it. 'Your father used to say that it's always the way with business – it's either difficult or it's good. So one doesn't talk about business. If business is good, people ask you for money. If business is bad, no one will lend you any money.' She paused. 'Anyway, how do you like my roast beef?'

*

So I had left my mother in Île d'Oléron, and was in Paris alone, which was to be neither the safest nor the most settled period of my life. Joining the new school, mid-term, was disastrous. I had no idea about the curriculum, especially when it came to maths, physics and chemistry; subjects I was pretty poor at, but had managed while at boarding school. My schoolwork was abysmal.

My loneliness, living by myself in a hotel room in the capital, was broken by visits to family friends, to be fed or given a bit of cash. There was a cinema beside the hotel, and I got to know the concierge and cleaner. He had a little garage room where he cooked on a camper's *Gaz* bottle, and he'd invite me for lunch. I'd bring the baguette and he'd share his tinned cassoulet. In the evenings he'd let me watch films in the cinema, and I found a girlfriend (it was a very innocent relationship) and I'd invite her to the cinema, which was free of charge – contacts!

I had little money, so thankfully I was sufficiently nourished by the hot chocolate and biscuits from Dr Stain's maid. I would drink and eat as Dr Stain (I was not allowed to call him Léon) told me stories about my father. He had a Romanian girlfriend but they never married. I had lunches at Goldenberg's restaurant, cassoulet and hand-outs from the concierge, and dinners with Aunt Juliette. They gave me some money or treated me to supper but, really, nobody looked after me, that little boy. They all had large, comfortable homes, but none said, 'You're only sixteen. You can't live alone in Paris. Let me do something for you because you can't be on your own.'

Being in Paris meant I could see a lot of friends I'd made during the holidays. They were mainly girls, of course. I also visited friends of my late father, who included the Mandorfs, a family who owned a large toy shop in Paris. I'd go to the shop where I'd help to pack presents, and enjoyed a few Sunday lunches at their home.

Danièle was one of the compassionate souls who fed me. Sometimes I'd visit her for dinner in the small flat where she lived with her two step-children and her husband, Jean-Claude Labb. She worked with the well-known producer, Denise Glaser, who had created and presented *Discorama*, the popular show that continued to be broadcast right up until the mid-70s. Through her work, Danièle had amassed thousands of records and, with a touch of entrepreneurial spirit, I said, 'Danièle, why don't I try to sell them? We could split the takings, fifty-fifty. What do you reckon?'

'I'm very happy with that,' she said. Did she do it to help me out? Or did she need the money? I don't know, but I think it was the former. And so began my career as a record salesman. I'd go regularly to Danièle's small flat with a huge suitcase and then pack it with records. On Sunday mornings, off I went, lugging the large case on the Metro and to the *marché aux puces* (the flea market). I'd get there for around 7am, early enough to find a free pitch. The market had pitches which required a payment, which I couldn't afford as I didn't have money. I asked other pitch holders if I could be on the corner of their pitch and in return, I'd give them some cash once I'd sold the records. They agreed.

I was very happy and it worked well. I can't remember how much I made, but do recall being proud that I was able to return to Danièle's and hand her half of the profits. And then I'd do it all over again, the following weekend.

I found another flea market which was open on Saturdays, so I went there too, which doubled my weekend sales. I was in the money (not much, but my ambitions were driven by two considerations: the ability to buy food and scrounging less from various people).

I was still living in the hotel and got to know another guy, an Italian, who may well have been in his early twenties. I'll call him Mario, as I seem to have erased his real name from my memory. I told Mario about my new career as a record salesman, and he said, 'Why don't I join you? I can come and help you sell the records.' We'd be able to carry twice as many suitcases (two), sell twice as many records, make twice as much money, and I'd have a companion so wouldn't get lonely.

'What a great idea, Mario,' I said. 'I like it. You're on!'

That Saturday and Sunday were brilliant. We did a very good job. Then he asked, 'Can you lend me some money, please? I'll pay you back tomorrow. And I'll pay you back double what you lend me.' He wanted to borrow all of our takings.

Well, my eyes flashed franc signs. I could see twice the amount of money, and visualised myself announcing to Danièle, 'I've made double the cash.' She'd be so proud of me. Well, the next evening I arrived at the hotel and asked for Mario.

'Ah, Mario has left the hotel.'

'Oh. Do you have an address for him?' I asked, almost knowing that the response would be no.

'No.'

It was early 1966 and I was just seventeen. Strangely enough, flash forward twenty-six years and I would be leading a management buyout for £25 million, with the support of twelve banks and trade finance lines of £75 million. I did not put my early experience on my CV, nor did I put some other similar experiences that happened in 1974.

*

During my time in Paris I managed to trace a childhood girlfriend, Roselyne. I'd met her years earlier in Berck, and now she was at boarding school, north of Paris. Our romance began through correspondence, a stream of love letters, flowing with great anticipation, until we met for a picnic, not far from her school. Suffice to say, the picnic was so enjoyable that next, I was invited to meet her parents in Abbeville. Then I told my mother, 'I want Roselyne to come to La Brée for the month of August.' Maman agreed.

My mother had encountered a few financial difficulties in paying for the hotel, so I moved to the small flat that was occupied by the cinema's concierge. I stayed for about a week, sleeping on a camp bed, and then I left school and returned to Île d'Oléron, probably in June or early July. My studies were over. My *baccalauréat* – or rather, no *baccalauréat* – was done.

It was the summer of 1966 when I left Paris and returned to La Bonne Auberge, and the start of the season. There was the beach, volleyball, fun to be had, and the World Cup to watch on television. To add to the excitement, I could await Roselyne's arrival.

I am thinking back now to that summer, and the assortment of characters at La Bonne Auberge. My mother had hired a student. He was also called Patrice. There was a German student, Ulla, who was working as a waitress, along with a few other young members of staff. They'd all come for the summer, known in hospitality as "the season". René the rotund chef returned for a second summer. John, the English soldier who had deserted the army, and whom we believed would never return to La Bonne Auberge, had, in fact, returned to La Bonne Auberge. About a year after he was escorted away by British military policemen, he had reappeared, greeting my mother with something like, 'Don't suppose I could have my old job back?'

John was restored to familiar territory, at the sink in the kitchen and washing up. Norma, who was now living in Bristol, had come back for a few weeks, and she was helping out. All hands were on deck. There was so little room at the inn that at night-time I shared a tent with John. Which at some point he may have shared with Ulla, the waitress. Before the season was done, she was pregnant and John the deserter was the dad.

Roselyne was due to arrive soon, but then... but then I met Angela. She came from the English town of Chichester, and was holidaying with a French family. After a short time with Angela, I was no longer looking forward to having Roselyne to stay for a day, or a week or, obviously, for a month. And shortly after England beat Germany to win the World Cup, Roselyne arrived. How fortunate that Patrice, my namesake, fancied Roselyne, and I think Roselyne was happy with Patrice.

The chef fell in love with one of the guests. She was married and with her husband. René was drunk at the bar, having dented our supplies of Ricard, as the husband abruptly departed. And I'm not sure he settled the bill. The chef also departed abruptly, half-way through the season. Now it was as if the furniture was being rearranged. My mother, good cook that she was, became the chef. Ulla and John, once lovers, no longer spoke to one another. Roselyne didn't stay a month. Norma and I served for the rest of the season, and Martini Man was still around.

Before too long, however, Norma the Nomad was preoccupied and restless once more. She missed Michael, and declared that she was fed up with Île d'Oléron. 'I'm going to live in Bristol,' she said. Having been back in France for about a year, she intended to start afresh in England's West Country, where she could await Michael's release.

'Why don't you come too?' she asked me. Bristol could be an adventure, I thought, and I would be with the half-sister I adored and admired. I said, 'Yes, I would love to come with you.' I had just made what would turn out to be the best decision of my life. Had I said no, I would never have met Liz.

Small issue: we needed new passports. My mother said she knew someone in Paris who could speed up the passports. At this time, she was unaware of Norma's intention to return to Bristol and, therefore, of our joint plan to go to Bristol. But we did not trust her. We saved cash from our tips and applied via the main town, Rochefort. A few weeks later we had our passports. With the season over, Norma went to Bristol ahead of me, settled herself in a flat and found a job as a sales assistant in a clothes shop. I was left with my mother, in an empty hotel. I had left school, had no job, and nowhere to go. It was quite a sad situation, and the hotel was in financial disarray.

Seventeen

The Bristol Act

My life in Britain began on 25th October, 1966. I did not know then that I would still be here now. I arrived, aged seventeen, to a nation chattering about the double agent George Blake and his escape from Wormwood Scrubs. Three days before I set foot on British soil, he had stepped off it. So much for high security. (Blake, too, crossed the Channel, but going in the opposite direction to me, and on his way to a safe haven in Moscow.)

I cannot remember how I broke the news to my mother that I would join Norma in Bristol, but I do recall her driving me from L'Île d'Oléron to Paris, and then taking me to Orly Airport, where I took a flight to Bristol. And I remember feeling the guilt of leaving her on her own. Norma met me at Bristol airport. I was so excited to see her, to forge a new life in Bristol and, possibly, to see Angela.

Norma took me to our new home, the basement flat at 62, Alma Road, which is close to Clifton Down railway station, Bristol Zoo, and the BBC headquarters. The flat had one bedroom, a living room, a kitchen, a bathroom, and a garden with a shed. Winter was just around the corner but there were only two electric heaters in the flat, each with only a single element. The weekly rent was £3, but the flat had a garage which we sublet for ten shillings. (A glimpse at the 2020 rental market, and I see that a one-bedroom flat in Clifton commands about £250 a week.)

Norma did not have a work permit but was in Britain on a visitor's permit. She had found a job in a clothes shop and was paid in cash, which kept everything simple for all concerned. No nasty book-keeping and tax forms. The shop was owned by a couple, a husband and wife, Frank and Annie Stacey. I have one particular memory of them, when they invited Norma and me to their home for supper. During the course of the evening, the wife, quite a bit older than me, began to kiss me and this turned to heavy petting. Norma was receiving the same attention from the husband. Norma was not pleased and we left the couple's home, abruptly. She kept the job but we were never again invited to theirs for "supper".

I was in Britain on condition of a student visa, and intended to be a student in Bristol – and I shall come to that subject. But first let me tell you a little about earning money in this great city of Gloucestershire. For a week I was a labourer for Frank Stacey, Norma's boss, who had bought a house to let, and needed some building work. This job involved digging soil from a back garden and transporting it by wheelbarrow to the front garden; wheeling bricks and stones from the back to the front; pouring cement from a mixer and then spreading it before laying the stones to create a drive at the front of the house. There were tea breaks of sweet PG Tips and sugary doughnuts, and lunches of fried eggs, sausage and bacon at a greasy spoon cafe. My salary: ten shillings a day, plus tea, doughnuts and greasy lunches at the greasy spoon.

For a month I worked as a teaching assistant at a local school, and liked teaching French to the pupils. When it came to being paid, however, there was a problem. The headmaster said, 'I'm sorry, I can't get the funding to pay for you as you don't have a work permit.'

As I had enjoyed teaching so much, I thought I'd advertise by putting a card in a newsagent's shop window: 'French lessons. Call Patrice.' This too, was not a successful way to earn money. To those in the know, which didn't include me, "French lessons" is a euphemism for prostitution. Put it on an ad in a shop window at your peril. I got lots of telephone calls and knocks on the door from men who thought that Patrice was a girl's name. 'Patrice? That's me,' I'd say cheerfully. They made their excuses and hung up or left.

Struggling financially – OK, we were skint – Norma and I resorted to shoplifting, and I mastered a certain technique for stealing. I'd wear a coat into the shop and, this way, could hide a steak under one arm – it was sort of snuggled into the armpit – and press an arm against the body to prevent the steak slipping out. The other armpit was ideal for a wedge of Edam – what is a Frenchman without his cheese? – again, pressing an arm against the body to stop the cheese dropping to the floor. Holding a loaf of bread with both hands in front of my body, I'd smile sweetly at the lady at the till. It took a while to conquer this trick, but in time I was adept, I am sorry to say, and was never caught, I am happy to say. (If you have ever wondered about the purpose of an armpit, well then, now you know.)

Also, doorstep deliveries of milk were commonplace (as were smutty jokes about milkmen and housewives). Norma and I would *borrow* milk from our near-but-not-too-near neighbours, a bottle from here, and then a bottle from there.

*

Keen to earn money, I would scour the jobs ads in newspapers. I saw this one: 'Are you a good salesman? If so, apply.' I applied. And I got the job, which was as a door-to-door salesman, selling children's encyclopaedias.

In those post-war years, and up to the mid-70s, children's

encyclopaedias were big business. Many British parents and grandparents bought the books as a collection for their kids and grandchildren. Appealingly, the cost amounted to only a few shillings a week and this was spread over months or even years. It was a perfect fit in the era when shoppers collected Green Shield Stamps and invested in premium bonds.

My employers were Pergamon Press, which was co-owned by Robert Maxwell, the newspaper tycoon. Three of us would be picked up by our boss and then driven to towns and villages on the outskirts of Bristol and, over the River Severn, in Wales. Often, we were dropped at council estates ("the target") where we'd look for houses with children. By which I mean we would look for houses with signs of children – outside the homes there would be prams, children's bikes or toys on the doorstep, or infants' clothes hanging on the washing line.

Next, I'd knock on the door and deliver the salesman's patter to the woman – the child's mother – who answered. 'Hello, I am doing a survey in the area, promoting education for children from four to twelve. I would welcome the opportunity of showing the survey to you and your husband. I'm only here for the day. Would it be feasible to see you after your dinner? By the way, your little boy looks absolutely gorgeous. How old is he? Oh, really? He looks so much older. And so bright. Just like his mother.'

It usually worked. I'd return later, meet the husband – fingers crossed, he didn't slam the door in my face – and tell both parents that I was conducting the survey as part of a government initiative, which was a lie, and that I had with me some sample literature. Perhaps the wife would be kind enough to make tea, and even serve biscuits. I'd produce a sample copy of the volume of encyclopaedias, with its stories, pictures, history, geography. The book was hefty and filled with colourful pictures of foreign lands, intriguing to these people who had rarely, if ever, been abroad on a plane.

I'd continue with the pitch: 'It's always a very difficult decision to budget for education, but you would agree that loving our children means also providing them with the best chances. Maybe if our parents had done that, we'd be in a better situation today.' I suppose this final point was central to the times, the 1960s. These people – the very nice couple listening to my pitch – had been children during the war. Chances were, they'd missed out on a good schooling. They did not want their children to suffer the same hardship, to be deprived of knowledge.

'The cost is five shillings a week,' I'd say. 'What's that? What does that amount to? The cost of two packets of cigarettes per week? So it's just a few cigarettes less each day...' Most people smoked in those days.

Two out of three visits resulted in a sale. Afterwards I'd meet my colleagues in a pub for a pint or two and a packet of crisps, and then I'd be home at about midnight, shattered. I did that job for six months, during which time there were some doors slammed in my face by angry husbands. Mostly, these people were poor and had very few opportunities in life. So when I look back on that job, I reckon it was probably the lowest thing I have done. Often, I wish I could meet them again, not to take their money but to repay them, with plenty of interest.

*

Norma and I lived together in Bristol for more than a year, visiting Michael in prison almost every Sunday. Then, on New Year's Day 1968, in the days when there was always a red box – a public telephone box – within walking distance, Norma and I walked to the nearest red telephone box. We wanted to call our mother in France, to wish her a happy new year. Often conversations with our mother had strange consequences, and this one was no exception.

We heard her speak down the telephone line, but only just. Her voice was strained and weak, which was not entirely unknown for her, but still, we were concerned and hundreds of miles from her.

'What's wrong, Maman?'

'I have sciatica,' she said. Our mother could always diagnose her illnesses. 'I can't move. I need one of you to come home and take me to a hospital in Paris.' She was in Île d'Oléron.

After the phone call, Norma and I discussed the possible options. Should Norma go? Should it be me? 'Actually, I've got no choice,' she said. 'I'll have to go, but I'm worried about leaving you alone in Bristol.' Norma left, and I can see her face now as she looked at me and delivered those parting words: 'I'll come back.'

I was alone. I did not want to go back to France because, in those twelve months in Bristol I was – at least in my opinion – doing well at Bristol University.

Being alone meant that I was now responsible for paying for the rent, cleaning the flat, doing the washing up, and I'd need coins for the launderette. Apart from feeding the electricity meter, I'd have to feed myself. All of this meant that inevitably I would need to find a job.

I went from one restaurant to another to see if there was any work. Amid the Georgian and Victorian buildings on Whiteladies Road, not far from my flat in Clifton, I came to a French restaurant, and popped in to see if they might have a job for me. Le Gourmet was owned by Tessa, a Scottish lady, and her husband, Jean-Claude (hence the French influence; he was probably le gourmet of Le Gourmet). The three of us chatted, I probably told them about my work experience at La Bonne Auberge, I am French, I like my food, they liked me, and sure enough I was appointed as the restaurant's new washer-up.

I was delighted to have an income, and soon realised that this job came with previously unexpected rewards: when the waitress brought dishes from the dining room, through the swing doors, and into the kitchen, I would swiftly devour the left-overs before plunging each plate into the basin of hot, soapy water. As the kitchen scavenger, my favourite was the fillet of steak au poivre with frites (even if the steak was overdone to please the British tastes of the sixties).

Jean-Claude was friendly and we joked a lot. Soon I was helping in the restaurant's bar and serving at the tables before zooming back to the kitchen to work – and eat – my way through the accumulated mountains of plates waiting to be washed. I learned how to make cocktails, and Irish coffee – an after-dinner favourite in those days. At the door, I welcomed guests, making them feel at ease as I showed them to their tables. If Jean-Claude wanted me to recommend certain dishes, I could do that too. I earnt bonus points from JC if I persuaded all the guests on the same table to order the same thing.

The restaurant's staff included two waitresses; two young ladies who'd come through that swing door with left-overs for me to devour rapidly like a slurping hyena. One of the waitresses was Irish and blonde. The other was dark-haired and busty. After service, JC would waggle the keys to his MG, and say to the Irish, blonde waitress, 'I'll run you home.' He was a really good boss like that. And off they'd go. My eyes were focused on the dark-haired busty waitress, though I had yet to own a car.

Although I did learn to drive while working at Le Gourmet. I passed my driving test on the third attempt. (On the first attempt I drove too fast. On the second, I did not fully appreciate the emergency brake, and stopped by a zebra crossing.) JC gave me an advance on my wages of £25 and I bought a car. It was green and I was extremely proud of it, but it was described by everyone else as "a jalopy" (Oxford English Dictionary definition: an old car in decrepit condition).

*

As for my life as a student... on arriving in Bristol I had planned to continue in higher education, and I adopted a morning routine.

First, I'd go to the university's student union building where I'd have a coffee and two doughnuts. (After working with Frank, I'd developed a taste for doughnuts.) 'I'll only charge you for one, love,' the elderly cashier would always say. She was good-natured and had taken a shine to me. After the sugar overload, I'd make the ten-minute stroll to Bristol library, down Park Street all the way, and in the building's basement I'd sit and read that day's newspapers.

During that time I met many French students. They were there to learn English, and became assistant teachers while studying at university. And I met many British students. So when I was not working, I developed a pretty good social life. There was the stock question from those I met: 'What are you studying?'

And then there was my stock response: 'I passed my *baccalauréat* in Paris. And now here I am, studying international law.' In truth, these statements were lies, fiction.

I wrote to Monsieur Perrier, my English teacher in Paris at Lycée Henri IV. He had known me from the age of eleven to thirteen, a period when I was a good student. I wrote something along the lines of, 'I am writing to you from Bristol, where I have decided to go to university. I am delighted to say that I passed my *baccalauréat*, and in order to be accepted onto the course, I require a letter of reference. Would you be so kind as to write that letter? I would be so very grateful.'

Monsieur Perrier responded quickly, providing a fantastic reference. Equipped with these words of praise, I applied to read sociology at the University of Bristol. If accepted, not only would I have a productive way of passing the time, but student status would also enable me to have a student visa. At that time I was in fact living in Britain with a temporary student visa but was not in fact a student.

My interview at the university was not especially successful, mostly because I had applied to study sociology when I did not know what sociology was. The department head asked me, 'What do you know about sociology?' As if that question wasn't bad enough, it was quickly followed by, 'And why do you want to study it?' Both were perfectly good questions given the circumstances, but they rendered me speechless, and for the rest of the interview I sat mostly in trance-like silence. I received a polite letter: 'Dear Mr Saiman, I am extremely sorry to say that your application has been declined. However, it was a pleasure to meet you and I would like to take this opportunity of wishing you the very best of luck.'

Unperturbed by the rejection of one department, I remained positive and determined to become a student – an undergraduate – even if that meant I was not officially recognised as a student. I would be a student, by my terms rather than the terms of the people who decided who should or shouldn't be allowed to study at the university.

With notepads and pens, I appointed myself as a student, and began as an undergraduate at Bristol University, first by attending lectures in politics and also in history. Then I went to any lectures that happened to interest me. There were no checks regarding those who attended lectures: it was easy to pretend to be a student. I lived as a student, I was among students, I argued as a student, so I was a student (just not officially).

One day, during politics, the lecturer invited the students to read a passage from Machiavelli's *The Prince*. Which I did, and I really threw myself into it. At the lecture the following week, there were questions on Machiavelli's book, and one of the students (*c'est moi*) could answer all the questions and raised plenty of issues with regard to modern-day politics. The lecturer invited a dozen students to a tutorial and – guess what? – I put my hand up and became one of the chosen few.

During the weekly tutorials we were asked to write essays which would be marked towards our degree (obviously not mine, as I wasn't registered). However, I read everything I could find on Machiavelli, and devoted myself to writing an essay about *The*

Prince. The following week the lecturer returned my paper and I was overjoyed to see he'd awarded me an A-plus. This lasted for six, or was it eight, tutorials.

I also went to lectures on English drama, where I learnt about Shakespeare, and then I joined the University's Dramatic Society.

Remember how I had lived a harmless lie when I pretended, as a young boy, that Maurice was my father. I had got in some practice then, had become convincing at pretence. Now I was living another white-ish lie, a life of make-believe, and I was credible, plausible. This was *my* fantasy. No one was harmed and it gave me immense pleasure. Some years earlier, in Lebanon, I had fallen in love with acting. I had dreamt of taking up a career in acting – before my mother arrived and took me back to Paris.

I absolutely loved acting. Now here I was, in the peculiar position of acting the part of a student being an actor. The members of my audience were the people I mixed with every day – friends, students, lecturers, the cashier at the till who saw me every morning and only charged me for one doughnut. All of them were participating unwittingly in this evolving piece of theatre. I had found – no, I had actually created – an existence that I wanted. I had found the freedom that was necessary to my survival.

What comes to mind is an observation made by a late, great actor. And he is someone who never knew his father. Peter Finch, the British-born movie star, was talking about the fascination, the magnetic draw of acting when he said, 'No one lives more lives than the actor.'

Eighteen

The Lunch that Changed Life

Around about the time Peter Finch was in front of the cameras, filming *Far From the Madding Crowd*, his daughter Anita was studying drama and on a stage at Bristol University. I know this because I too was on that same stage.

I was a friend of Anita, who was the daughter of Peter by his marriage to the ballet dancer, Tamara Tchinarova (Anita was nine when her parents divorced, after Tamara discovered that Peter was having an affair with Vivien Leigh). In the university's Winston Hall, we appeared together in Stuart Olesker's play, *The Forest and Brother Daedalus*. I was Brother Lazarus, a lead role. (After university, Anita went on to play a few minor parts in British television series, such as *Target* with Patrick Mower, and later she moved to Spain.)

We also performed in a production of four medieval farces: in *La Jalousie du Barbouillé* (attributed to Molière), I had the lead as Le Barbouillé. My (character's) poor wife was played by Hélène Davin-Turcat. She was the niece of Major André Turcat, whose name may not be familiar but he was a hero of aviation. In March

1969 – two years almost to the very day after our production – Major Turcat test piloted Concorde's first prototype.

Anyhow, performing on stage encouraged me to consider resuming my career as an actor, and I applied to the highly-respected and long-established Bristol Old Vic Theatre School. I passed the first audition but was not a good dancer, and, on reflection, the British public was not ready for a Shakespearean actor with a genuine French accent. Although I had rehearsed a speech by Lord Capulet, and still know the first lines.

I was so entrenched in university life that one day I went to the administration office and simply asked for a certificate to verify that I was in full-time studies, reading English at the University of Bristol. Luckily, I knew one of the girls who worked in that department and she found me quite charming. So much so, that she sorted out the certificate and had it signed by the dean of the university. This certificate enabled me to acquire a foreign student's visa, which meant I could stay in Britain. The certificate was also the route to a student card which, in turn, gave me access to the refectory. Warming even more to my student theme, I joined Bristol University's volleyball team. I had progressed from acting as a student, to acting as a volleyball player and was so convincing that I got the lead role – I became captain of the team. We played in matches, home and away, against the teams of other universities and there I was, peculiarly the sporty ambassador of the university that had – officially – rejected my application.

I was a student without having to sit exams and I was learning as much as I could in whatever subject I chose. Each lecture provided a new opportunity to absorb knowledge and, come the evening, I'd earn cash and eat well on the left-overs at Le Gourmet – except for Mondays, when I had the night off work, and would try to find a date for that evening.

*

Although I did not wish to return to France, my mind often took me back there. Among the memories there was a powerful recollection of an afternoon in November 1963, a few weeks before my fifteenth birthday. My mother and I were at La Bonne Auberge at the time, and we sat together to watch the funeral of John F Kennedy. I was struck by the sight of John Kennedy Junior standing at his mother's side. The assassination happened on 22nd November, and the funeral was taking place three days later, on the 25th. It was John junior's third birthday. The world was shocked and silenced by Kennedy's murder. The world was also united in grief, especially by the image of the fatherless child, John-John, at his mother Jackie's side, both watching as ceremoniously the stars and stripes flag was removed from the coffin lid, and folded, before the coffin was lowered.

It reminded me of my own situation, my own childhood, though John Kennedy Junior got to attend his father's funeral. The image of the president's little boy took me back to the death of my father, and it touched me deeply. Still today, I am moved when I see that footage.

Now, the photographer Stanley Tretick photographed Kennedy at the White House in October, the month before the assassination. Jackie did not like the couple's children to appear in photographs, for fear of being accused of using them for political gain. However, she wasn't at the White House on the day that Tretick came to take the pictures. Which meant that there was no one to object when Tretick wanted to take a few shots of John senior sitting on his desk in the Oval Office, while John-John, aged two, crawled and played in the footwell of the desk that the child called his "house".

These photographs were to be published in *Look* magazine. Actually, when the presidential parents made that ill-fated trip to Dallas, their luggage included an advance copy of the issue that featured the photos. Well, days after Kennedy was shot, the photographs came out and appeared in newspapers and other magazines all around the world. The moment I saw the images – the little boy under his father's desk – I was connected to the memory of being under my father's desk, crawling around and playing in what I called my "house".

Kennedy's death had intrigued me, though no more than any other curious soul might be intrigued. However, here in Bristol, I began to develop an obsession with his assassination. I read all that I could about his murder, spending entire days in the city's library. I befriended the head librarian, and he helped me by researching and then ordering numerous books on the subject, including Mark Lane's *Rush to Judgment*, which endorsed the conspiracy and that it was impossible for Oswald to have acted alone.

The librarian, thinking that I was a student, helpfully let me know about the arrival of the report by the Warren Commission: a document of 888 pages which concluded that JFK was shot by a lone gunman, Lee Harvey Oswald, who acted alone. There was no conspiracy, according to the commission.

There were unanswerable questions about life and death in my own existence. But these could be put to one side as I devoted myself – my energy, attention, concentration – to the unanswerable questions concerning the life and death of someone else, a stranger I felt I knew. I pored over every word of anything Kennedy-related, feeding an almost-insatiable appetite for solving the mystery.

I got hold of a copy of the Zapruder film, the 8mm colour motion picture of the assassination filmed by Abraham Zapruder on his Bell and Howell camera as the motorcade passed through Dallas. The sequence of frames shows the split second at which Kennedy was hit. I spent hours and hours writing a lengthy document about the assassination. I wrote it in English and then translated it into French, and I tried to get it published but there were no takers.

At that stage I could only come up with the conclusion that the Warren Commission, by concluding Oswald was the only assassin, had presented what was probably the most acceptable solution for the government. Any other conclusion might have involved conspiracy, and the possibility that the government was not capable of spotting the conspiracy. And where would that conspiracy have come from? Russia? Cuba? Today we still don't know.

The only thing we do know today is that it is less likely that Kennedy was killed by only one man, Oswald. It is more likely that there was a conspiracy. High on the list of possible conspirators is the Mafia. Both John and Bobby Kennedy had upset the Mafia by battling against organised crime. Oswald was there but, I reckon, it's highly unlikely he acted alone.

And what I do know is that one night a friend stayed over because he had drunk too much. I put him in my bed – to sleep! – but said, 'You stay on your side of the bed.' In the middle of the night, I came round and he was shaking me. He looked panicky as he shook me.

'Pat, wake up. Wake up.'

I said, 'What's wrong?'

He said, 'You really frightened me. You were talking in your sleep, saying, "The bullet came through the back of the head and went through the front…"' My ramblings were about Kennedy, but had a sobering effect on my friend in the bed.

The document remained with me for a while but then I shared a house with a friend and left it there. He moved house and, in the process, my Kennedy document – that labour of love – was lost, abandoned, thrown away, who knows?

*

And when my mind was not focused on America's crime of the century, I could give some time to that master criminal closer to home. I am talking of Michael, deprived of his liberty and serving his time at Leyhill Prison.

Norma had vowed to wait for Michael. Then she had returned to France to look after our mother and, as we said *au revoir*, Norma had added, 'I'll come back.' She did not. Could not. Although Norma had promised to wait for Michael to come out, it was now I who waited for Norma to come back.

She had intended to return, but this time decided to apply for a work permit. Her application set the alarm bells ringing. The British authorities saw from their records that she had been deported from the States, and had been the girlfriend of a certain Michael Alterman, currently serving time for fraud. She had been a headache to the Americans. Now Norma was a potential migraine for the British powers. 'Permit declined.' She remained in Paris, but she also found a good reason to stay there.

This left me to perform the duty of prison visitor. I would take the forty-five-minute bus journey from Bristol, heading north to the charming little parish of Tortworth, a village as famous for the ancient chestnut tree that sits in the churchyard of St Leonard's church. Not far from the village, you'll find the prison, which is set within a massive estate of gardens and a farm, which are tended by the inmates.

Those inmates, by the way, have included the novelist and former Tory party chairman, Jeffrey Archer. In the 1970s, a young man, Leslie Grantham, murdered a taxi driver in Germany and was sent to Leyhill. As an inmate, he took up acting and a passion was ignited. Acting is a way of living other's lives, which can help if your own one isn't great. About a decade after his release, Grantham became a household name, playing Dirty Den, the landlord of a pub in a new soap opera called *EastEnders*.

But staying in the late 1960s, I'd go to Leyhill to see Michael, the imprisoned partner of my absent half-sister. I'd take him packets of cigarettes and, in a cafeteria within the prison, we'd sit and chat, and he'd smoke, as other inmates served tea and always the same type of biscuits, chocolatey Bourbons. As for the meetings, they were all smiles and laughter, stiff upper lip stuff, and really quite jolly. He was a convicted conman, but conmen can be likeable, charming and entertaining.

It was difficult to visit the prison without hearing the same joke about how the prisoners were allowed to do any sports – except cross-country running. And usually Michael wouldn't let me leave without imparting advice that could see me through life, as if he was oblivious to his circumstances. He was hardly in a position to be the oracle, but during the ninety-minute visits, he'd deliver monologues beginning with 'Take my advice, Pat…' or, 'Let me give you a tip…' His tip tended to be that I should return to France. I was wise enough by then, I think, to trust my judgment above Michael's.

Then we'd shake hands and Michael would go off to prune the roses or lift potatoes on the farm, and I'd catch the bus back to Bristol, or maybe to shoplift for my next meal. One day I caught the bus and there was another passenger – a complete madman – who took against me because he presumed that I was an inmate on day release. 'Con,' he snarled, bringing his face close up to mine. 'I know where you come from…'

I didn't want him to think I was a convict. Other passengers were looking. 'No, no, no,' I said. 'I was just visiting someone in the prison.' But he was having none of it and persisted with the hassling. I asked the bus driver, 'Can I sit at the front, please? Near you.' Never has a young Parisian been more relieved to get off a bus than me when I reached my stop.

Then the prison visits came to an end. They stopped. Not because Michael left prison but because I left Bristol. I had moved to London, and was a salesman for Howard Cohen, travelling around England, selling non-stick pans and ironing board covers ("guaranteed for life") in department stores and markets in London's East End, such as Leather Lane. We'd go to agricultural shows, selling our wares. Polaroid sunglasses, fountain pens, bendy toys; we sold them all.

During those days of selling, I remember an irritated customer – and I don't know what I'd done to annoy him – called me "a fucking Jew". I was so amazingly pleased by this insult. I knew I was not Jewish by birth, but I was very proud about my father being Jewish. I had a star of David, and was working with Jewish people and felt very proud to be part of the Jewish community.

Yes, I was proud of my father and I was proud of that insult. I was proud that I was living in London, sharing a flat – at 21 Lancaster Grove, Swiss Cottage – with four other guys: two accountants, a trainee solicitor and an engineer. And I must say that I was bursting with pride when, before turning twenty, I bought my first car. It was a blue Ford Anglia, registration BOA 563.

*

In the autumn of 1969 Hélène's father, Major Turcat, flew Concorde on its maiden flight from Toulouse airport. And I drove to Dover in my blue Ford Anglia, parked the car, took a ferry to Calais, and from there took the coach to Paris.

I was back in the French capital because I wanted to find out about my father's will and intended to meet with the solicitor who held the document. Funds would become available to me when I reached the age of twenty-one, which was in December, a couple of months away.

Being back in France would enable me to catch up with my mother and Norma and during the trip I was invited to lunch by Albert Goldenberg. He was like a godfather to me, and we enjoyed each other's company. Albert could – would – tell me stories about the man I regarded as a god. He felt indebted to my father, especially because of that murder trial after the war. Apart from being best friends, Albert and my father had been business partners (my father invested in his deli) and were so close that, as I've previously said, they had a joint wedding. My father had named me Patrice.

Albert's son was Patrick, born a year earlier than me (and, by the way, circumcised on the counter of his father's deli).

The trial was firmly in the past when Albert and I met for lunch. He was known not for that case but as "the doyen of Jewish restaurateurs in Paris", playing host to, and feeding the stars of showbusiness, sport and politics. With his younger brother Jo, he had created an institution there in rue des Rosiers. That is where we had lunch on that particular day, at the bar of the deli in the place where my father had spent so much of his time... when he was not gambling. 'I loved your father,' Albert once said to me, 'but what I didn't love was that he gave me a love of the casinos.'

As we ate and drank, Albert asked, 'Patrice, tell me, what are you up to? What are you doing, workwise?'

I was proud of what I had achieved. I worked hard, was independent and even had my own car, which I regarded as an accomplishment. So it was with pride that I replied, 'Oh, I have been selling encyclopaedias and sunglasses... and ironing board covers. You name it, I sell it. I did washing-up in a restaurant. A French restaurant...' I could see that Albert was not sharing my enthusiasm. 'And I was a waiter at the same restaurant...'

Albert, restaurateur extraordinaire, looked utterly despondent. 'Patrice, your father would have liked you to do something else for a living. To have a proper career...'

'That's all very well,' I said, shocked and angry, 'but I have no *baccalauréat*, no degree and no idea how to find a proper career.'

Albert had a solution. 'When you get back to London, go and meet a friend. His name is Jean Lemberger. I'd like you to meet him.'

'Yes, of course, Albert.'

He told me some more about Jean and the company he worked for, which was in international trade. Then he said, 'Good. I'll call him and then you can arrange an appointment.' We left the restaurant and walked to Albert's apartment as he wanted to give me shirts and a leather jacket (that didn't fit), and he insisted I take some cash. A couple of years later, in 1971, Albert would sell the restaurant in rue des Rosiers to his younger brother Jo, while he opened another restaurant, at 69 Avenue de Wagram, a nice stroll from the Champs-Elysées.

*

Jean Lemberger was one of the directors of Leopold Lazarus. It was the British arm of the Lissauer group, a business that traded in steel and metals, and had offices around the world. Although Albert had urged me to see Mr Lemberger, it was really Albert's brother Simon who had enabled the introduction. Simon ran the company's office in East Berlin, to where he had fled before the murder trial after the war.

Mr Lemberger gave me a warm welcome. 'Now, what's all this, young man? Albert Goldenberg says you are looking for a job...' I took Mr Lemberger through my career to date. Essentially, it illustrated that I knew nothing except surviving but I added, 'All I want is an opportunity to learn a job.' Lemberger had left school at sixteen and had survived the war. He was very keen on helping young people like me.

He sent me to Mr Killy, the company's personnel manager, who had the air of a strict, rather unpleasant headmaster, and came straight to the point: 'Are you good at maths?'

'I am. Absolutely. Yes. It was my favourite subject at school.' (If he'd asked about nuclear physics, he'd have got an equally effusive response.) I forgot to say to him that I had been brought up with the metric system in France, while Britain was trading in the imperial system. The currency was in pounds, shilling and pence. Tonnages were in long tonnes, quarter hundredweights and pounds. I sat a test that required lots of conversion charts, and I may as well have been taking an exam in Mandarin. I was given a peculiar calculating machine to make the conversions from metric to imperial, and convert currencies to sterling. I was also given a couple of sheets of conversion charts. That was my introduction to the imperial system against the metric system. No need to continue except to say that I had no idea what to do.

I failed the tests, went into a toilet cubicle and cried, and then went back to see Mr Lemberger in his office. I blamed the silly, out-dated imperial system for my dismal efforts. It didn't matter. 'You've got the job, Patrice,' he said. 'Well done.' Hmm. I was confused, but delighted. Clearly, Mr Killy's opinion had not been taken into account. (Later on, whenever I passed him in the corridor, I got a sense of the injustice he felt towards me; that I had been given a job I did not deserve.)

I started the following day, working as a trainee – lackey – in Saul Goodman's office, on a monthly salary of about £50. Saul was a lovely man and in charge of administration at the company. Pam was the battleaxe who worked for him as his assistant, and I feared her from the beginning. I had to learn how to create invoices using the imperial system and these were checked by ferocious Pam. After a fortnight of hard work – late nights, early mornings and weekend practice – I had mastered the art. More than that, I became Pam and Saul Goodman's pet, and was their ever-cheerful tea boy, and happy to throw myself into any task, no matter how menial.

I was given the chore of chasing customers for money, if only so that I could hear one of the four familiar responses: the cheque's in the post; I paid yesterday; the amount is wrong; the date of the invoice is wrong.

During that period I also learned about shipping. However, my first decision on shipping was made in a lunch hour when everyone else in the office had gone for something to eat. I answered the phone to a shipping agent in Antwerp, and he asked me about a particular ship's bill of lading (this is a detailed list of a ship's cargo in the form of a receipt given by the master of the ship to the person consigning the goods). Confidently, I replied on behalf of the shipping manager that there was no problem about making changes, but then I forgot to mention this call to the shipping manager, Mr Bolt, aptly named for the metals industry. My memory was only jogged when I heard Mr Bolt screaming with anger after a telex arrived from the shipping agent, mentioning the bills of lading with my agreed changes. Mr Bolt tore me to pieces, documents had to be returned to Belgium and new documents had to be issued. I still had a job. Though I had no idea how I still had a job, except that Saul and Pam were supportive.

*

I was two months into the job when I received a letter from the French consulate. The letter informed me that I had been drafted into the French army. I had been assigned to the parachute regiment, and would be required to attend camp in thirty days' time. I was to be based in Perpignan, in the south-west of France.

In France it was compulsory for young men to do twelve months' National Service. This, of course, I knew. However, I lived in Britain not in France, and presumed that the letter was a piece of humorous fiction, even if it was written on official notepaper. I thought, I'm being set up as the victim of a practical joke. Then I thought, OK, hang on, maybe it's best to go to the consulate just to double check. Which I did, and that is where and when I learnt that, actually, the letter was not a practical joke.

I said, 'I've just started a job. I don't have any money to go back to Toulouse. I don't know anyone in Toulouse. I'd rather stick to the job and forget about the army.' If I refused to return for National Service, said the man at the consulate, I would be arrested when I next set foot on French soil. The man was adamant: 'We don't care about your new job. You must join the army.'

He made a couple of concessions. One, I would be able to

transfer to the *Infanterie de Marine* who were based in Melun, an hour by train from Paris. Two, my start date would be postponed by a couple of months, to early January 1970. 'Oh, and don't worry about finding the money to travel to France. We'll pay for your fare.' Back at the office I was upset, and broke the news to Mr Lemberger. 'Don't worry,' he said, ever the good guy. 'Go to France. Try to get out of the army as quickly as possible. And you'll still have a job here upon your return.'

Nineteen

Patricia

So often extraordinary things happen in ordinary moments. An incident comes to mind and it concerns a lady called Marianne Martin. As a single woman in her twenties, she had lived in Paris after the war. She was now approaching fifty, was a mother of four, and lived in north-east France, in the city of Strasbourg. She was at home one day, standing at the ironing board and pressing clothes as she listened to the radio. It was a very ordinary moment in Madame Martin's life. The extraordinary thing was about to come.

About a month earlier I had been in Paris. It was my visit in the autumn of 1969, you'll recall, when I had lunch with Albert Goldenberg. That lunch when he had changed the course of my career and, ultimately, the course of my life. But I had gone to Paris primarily to see the solicitor about my father's estate. I was the main beneficiary and due to inherit in a couple of months when I turned twenty-one.

I remember it well. The notary and I sat in his office – him on one side of the leather-topped, mahogany desk, me, *le jeune*

145

homme, on the other. He began to explain the situation regarding the estate, and my late father's wishes. 'We do have a file,' he said, 'but we have not had any instructions for investment.' In other words, my father's money had been idle, earning nothing, which was irritating. (I'd also thought that Maurice had advised on investment, but clearly that was not the case.)

'So what was there at the time of your father's death in 1953 is the money that is there today... less our fees.' Today I would have sued that firm of solicitors.

'Now, Patrice, you are the main beneficiary,' he continued. My father had left me everything. From memory, this amounted, in the equivalent of British money, to two or three thousand pounds. Which, of course, would have been worth more in 1953 than it was in 1969. And as it had been idle, it was worth less in 1969 than in 1953. The rest of the estate had diminished. For instance, I would have inherited his apartment, but my mother had sold it soon after his death and the proceeds were long since spent.

'We will have a problem in distributing the funds,' said the solicitor.

'A problem?'

'Yes, although you are the main beneficiary it does not mean you will receive all of the money. Under French law, you see, a certain amount must be set aside for all of your father's children, irrespective of his wishes. This means that Danièle is a beneficiary. And also, your half-sister, Patricia.'

During my childhood, I knew that I had another half-sister. But I had never met or spoken to her. In fact, even though I was aware of Patricia, I have no recollection of discussing her with either my mother or Norma. Now – and in order to receive my inheritance – I would have to find my unknown half-sister. The solicitor offered to try to track down Patricia, but it would only serve to increase his fees, and to avoid paying him even more, I said, 'Don't worry. Leave it to me. I'll find her.'

In truth, I did not reckon I would be able to locate Patricia. Her surname was as common in France as Smith or Jones in Britain. And remember, this was '69, so there was no internet to help with the search (and six years before the two co-founders of Google were born). But when I returned to London, I wrote to the radio station, France Inter, to place an ad that would be read out on air; an appeal for Patricia to get in touch with me.

My father's weaknesses were not limited to the casino, as Albert had suggested to me. After the war, when he was in his forties, my father dedicated a good deal of his time to women, preferably beautiful ones who were in their twenties. His womanising was a frequent source of fights between him and Danièle, and the reason that she moved out of his apartment. She grew tired of answering the door to a stream of my father's lovers, who were just a few years older than her.

And it was one of those lovers, Marianne Le Berre, who became pregnant. On 17th April, 1947, she gave birth to a daughter, Patricia-Carole, in St-Denis, the northern suburb of Paris. That was around the time Raoul, my father, met Marcelle, my mother, on that night when Raoul's car apparently broke down within walking distance of his apartment.

And moving forward a couple of decades, Marianne Martin (née Le Berre) was at home in Strasbourg and performing the ordinary chore of ironing, when she stopped suddenly as she heard an extraordinary announcement on the radio: *'Patrice Saiman is trying to get in touch with his half-sister Patricia Martin. She is the daughter of Marianne Martin.'*

*

Shortly afterwards I received a letter: 'Dear Patrice, I am your sister, Patricia...' Marianne had phoned the radio station and was given my address. This she passed to her daughter Patricia, who was living in England. She shared a flat in Hampstead with a few other girls, and worked for an advertising agency. I was selling ironing board covers ("guaranteed for life"). I went to see her. I went to meet for the first time my half-sister.

There was an immediate warmth between us which was possibly due to the circumstances of the search. When I embarked on it, I did not really think I would find her and so never imagined that we would meet. The objective of finding Patricia was to have access to the remains of the estate, and I had not considered the relationship itself.

But we got on well. Two people who were from the same father with a joint history and yet each did not know the story of the other. And so, in her flat, we talked and talked. Patricia was able to tell me the story of her life and I told her the story of mine. Then I slept on the floor in her flat.

It was many years ago, but there is a part of her story that for both of us remains a vivid memory. Throughout her childhood and into her teens Patricia believed that the man she called 'Papa' was indeed her papa. His name was Pierre Martin, and he had married Marianne Le Berre after Patricia was born. And so my half-sister grew up as Patricia Martin. Her true origins became the ticking time bomb of the Martin's family secrets. The bomb exploded – the secret was out – appropriately enough during a row between mother and daughter, when Patricia was sixteen or seventeen. The subject of the argument is not remembered, but Patricia happened to say, 'Well, I am going to talk to my father about it…'

And Marianne, irritated and off balance, snapped back, 'Well, you can't talk to your father because your father is not your father. Your father is someone else.'

When Patricia had applied for a new passport, she required her birth certificate. At that point the next piece fitted in to this jigsaw that was her strange life. On the certificate, and beneath the space for the father's name, there it was: 'Salomon Raoul Saiman'. Just as it is on mine. When we met for the first time at her flat, she had known only for a few years the identity of her father.

*

Raoul, my father, two-timed Marianne by seeing Marcelle, the woman he would marry. Marianne two-timed Raoul by also seeing Pierre, the man she would marry. Patricia and I would continue to meet, and sometimes talked about our father and what he saw in our mothers. What did her mother, Marianne, and Marcelle, my mother, have in common, aside from the fact that both had a child by Raoul? Both women were about the same age, which was about twenty years younger than my father had been. Both women were elegant, stylish, beautiful and sexy.

Both women had begun their relationships with my father after he had returned from the war, and from his travels which, as you know, took him to Brazil. While there he had bought the topaz. He had kept the reddish-orange stone with him for the remaining years of the war, as he moved from one country to another and finally, back in Paris, he had met my mother. In love and wanting to give something to his future wife, Raoul took the stone to a jeweller. The stone was mounted and presented as a ring to Marcelle. 'It's imperial topaz. The ring is unique,' he had told her. Bright, ostentatious and stunning, it was indeed spectacular.

At least, that was the story I knew until, one day I met Marianne. She told me lots of fantastic things about my father. 'And I must show you that I have a present from your father. I still have it.' She then showed me a ring, with a beautiful topaz stone. 'Your father gave it to me,' she said. 'And it is unique.' Our father had given to each of his lovers a jewel cut from the same large stone.

Topaz linked Marcelle and Marianne to my father, and it was certainly appropriate: the golden stone is regarded as a symbol of fertility.

Twenty

Crying for Help

As I write, Britain is in the midst of the great lockdown. In the third week of March the government told us to stay at home, save lives. So over recent months, a nation – much of the world, in fact – has been behind closed doors, helping to prevent the spread of the coronavirus, Covid-19.

Each of us has reacted differently. Our moods, our emotions, have not been in sync, of course. One day I might be feeling good, while you are feeling low. The next, I'll be feeling miserable and you'll be on top form.

Quite frankly, I felt wretched during those early couple of weeks of lockdown. I knew that a structured day would help see me through, it was the key to "survival". I struggled to find a routine, however. I struggled, partly because I craved my daily game of tennis, which is hardly the greatest hardship at a time of worldwide crisis, but mostly because the lockdown by its very nature had prevented freedom. Again, this affected each person differently. In my case, I was taken back to a couple of periods of my life when my freedom was snatched away, and I had been depressed...

There was that spell as a seven-year-old pupil at the boarding school in Vallée de Chevreuse, a short-lived experience but grim nevertheless. The lockdown also took me back fifty years to my stint of National Service in the French Army. It had begun on Monday, 5th January, 1970, shortly after I'd turned twenty-one and, as a reference point, it was the era when US series such as *M*A*S*H* and *Hawaii Five-0* were becoming popular.

Like boarding school at seven, my military experience was dreadful. I was plunged into a mental abyss so deep and dark that I could see no way out of it, and so, one day – hopeless and helpless – I tried to kill myself. I must emphasise that I did not contemplate suicide during those early days of lockdown – not for a moment – but sure, I was reminded of the sadness of that period, of being in the army. They were memories which I suppose I'd put in their own sort of lockdown decades ago.

*

I can see myself – a soldier, with a heavy heart, in the barracks and kitted out with everything I'd need. Our sergeant had a scar – a dent in his skull – caused by a bullet. 'Regardez! Regardez!' he'd say, urging us to look. He'd got it in Vietnam. All of us were convinced that his brain had been touched by the bullet, as he was a complete madman.

So I had no wish to do military service, had a sergeant who was crazy and then there was Brigitte. I was in love with Brigitte, and maybe the loneliness of the army amplified that so-called love: the army had torn us apart.

In these barracks in Melun, south of Paris, I was down-hearted from the start. We were dispatched to a building where we were handed uniforms, shoes, socks, shirts, jumpers, coats, berets, and then sent for crewcuts. Next, we were rushed – *'Allons! Vite!'* – to our barracks. 'Now, make your beds.' *'Allons! Vite encore!'* The hole-in-the-head sergeant shouted at us for whatever reason, or for no other reason than to make us feel more awful. By midday we were all on the barracks square, dressed up as soldiers on parade, and being told by a senior officer that each of us was hugely relevant to the progress of our nation. 'Do not underestimate how important you are to France,' declared the officer, a sea of young, green troops before him.

Then it was a case of adapting to the regimental routine. This comprised the following: spring out of bed at five every morning; make the bed, and then shave; hurry to the square for drill (shoulder-to-shoulder marching, in time with one another); breakfast. There were shooting classes, marching classes, and classes in which we learned how to hold our weapons. Each of us was given ten packets of Gauloises, those strong, punchy, macho cigarettes. I'd sell them because I did not smoke. We did not have smoking classes.

There were trips to Camp de Mourmelon, also known as Camp de Châlons. This military base is in Mourmelon-le-Grand, a few hours' drive towards the east of France, and built at the behest of Napoleon III in the 1850s. It was an air base for the Americans at the end of the Second World War. Our whole camp would get transported en masse to Mourmelon by Jeep and lorry, and once there we'd play war games with tanks and big, deafening guns. We'd also do target practice, and we'd run with our weapons, fall down at order, get up again and run with our weapons into water. It was pretty awful.

I learnt about radio communications, including the NATO-style alphabet – **Alpha**, **Bravo**, **Charlie** – and I was told that when we came to go on manoeuvres in a month's time, I'd be the radio officer in a lieutenant's Jeep, which was quite cosy compared with the long seats in the back of a lorry. Guard duty at night-time was awful, lasting from 8pm to 7am, in three-hour shifts. I listened to music on my little transistor radio, as I worried about how I'd get out of the army.

*

I considered the potential exit routes. To begin with, I claimed that I was a practising Jew and could only eat kosher food. That did not last long. They called the local rabbi to talk to me and he had an issue in establishing my orthodoxy. I dropped that idea, and concentrated on building a case that I was not physically fit.

In the first couple of weeks of training, each of us was sent for a medical at the infirmary. The doctor was a doctor in the real world, and a new recruit, like the rest of us. Here he was, serving his time in the army infirmary, and he turned out to be a very decent man. He asked, 'Do you have any injuries?'

'Yes, in fact I do,' I said. 'I sprained my ankle a couple of months ago.' That bit was true. Then I lied: 'It's still hurting a lot. I mean, really, really badly… and the army boots are extremely painful.'

He said he would be happy to send me for an X-ray and assessment and, a couple of days later, I squeezed myself onto a bench in the back of an army lorry that was crammed with poorly young recruits. We drove north to Paris, and to Val-de-Grâce, which was, until 2016, the grand and imposing military hospital in Paris. Here, we awaited our appointments. I saw another young doctor, and again I did the injured soldier act and was emphatic, 'I'm in agony with my foot. It's really hurting.'

An X-ray did not back up my claim – how could it? – but the doctor was compassionate. 'There's little case for giving you dispensation,' he said, 'but I'll give you a letter, and that'll get you out of having to wear army boots for three months.' This was great news. If I couldn't wear army boots then I would have to be excused from marches and runs. Better still, I would not be able to go on guard duty. Sure enough, back at barracks I was excused from many exercises and guard duty. Perfect.

The young doctor at the infirmary was on my side, and also explained the grading system which decides the fitness of a soldier to remain in the army. I was currently at a grade of P3. 'In order to get discharged you'd have to be P5,' he said. He added that if I wanted to pursue this grade, he would send me back a week or so later to Val-de-Grâce so that I could try again, have another stab at it. Yes, please.

Bootless and apparently disabled, I settled into my role as radio operator. This required me to sit – of course – in the back of a Jeep, behind a lieutenant and a driver. Being the radio operator was quite a cushy job and another radio operator gave me some advice to make the job even more cushy, if such a thing was possible. He said to me, 'If you don't want to use the radio you need to break the radio. So you put the three amp fuse in the five amp spot, and you put the five amp on the ten amp…'

'OK,' I said, listening intently as if being given the formula of a magical elixir.

'Then switch it on. Kaput! The radio won't work.' I thanked him, and then that's what I did. Three amp there, five amp there… switch on the radio… Kaput! Turn to lieutenant: 'Sorry, sir.'

On my friendly doctor's "advice", I returned to Val-de-Grâce, possibly confident that I would see the same ridiculously lenient doctor who had previously treated me. I reckon I did a commendable job of acting as I limped through the hospital courtyard, in the shadow of the statue of Dominique Jean Larrey, Napoleon's personal surgeon and considered to be the first modern military surgeon.

However, once inside, I was told that I had an appointment with a different doctor. He was probably in his sixties, impeccably resplendent in uniform, and his puffed-up chest was emblazoned with rows of glittering medals. If he was not a general then he was a captain. As I limped up to him, he barked, 'What's the matter with you?'

'Well, sir, I… it's my ankle…' I grimaced and winced. 'My foot, sir…'

He cut me off brusquely, waving a hand in the air – stop talking, shut up; I got the message. He pointed at a chair. I sat down. He held up the X-ray to the light of the window, and glanced at the picture of my lower leg; the tibia, fibula and talus. Then, still without saying a word to me, he took a piece of paper and I watched as he began to write a brief letter, the pen darting across the page. I can still see him, gleaming medals on chest, swishing pen in hand. What on earth was he writing? Once he had finished, he folded the paper, slid it into an envelope, licked the seal, sealed the envelope, turned it over and addressed it to the commander at the barracks where I was based. Then he handed the letter to me. 'Give this to your captain upon your return.' And that was an order. I saluted, turned, gave a couple of groans as if in pain, and limped away. And as I did so, I was thinking to myself, oh dear, this doesn't seem good at all. I found the nearest lavatory, locked myself in a cubicle and opened the letter that was for my captain's eyes only. The doctor had written:

'My dear commandant,

Have you not noticed that this young soldier is simply trying to get a discharge from the army?

I leave you to deal with him appropriately.'

What the hell. This letter was not going anywhere, I decided, and that was a fact of life. My life. Back at barracks, the young doctor said, 'How did you get on at Val-de-Grâce?'

'Oh, it was all right. The doctor said, stay as you are... no boots.'

'Do you have a letter?'

'Erm, no.'

*

My hands trembled as I read the letter from Brigitte. Throughout my youth all I had wanted to do was fall in love with somebody. Yes, I wanted to fall in love, to be in love; I really wanted to be with someone. True, I was quite desperate and would take an interest in almost any single girl. Brigitte had been keen on me, too. But then the French army happened to come along and it got in the way, and prevented us from seeing one another. I felt as if I was in jail and, as I contemplated a life of brief encounters with Brigitte, I sank lower and lower. And then came that morning when the post was being shared in the barracks, and I heard the shout, '*Saiman, un pour toi…*' My sweetheart, Brigitte, had written a Dear John letter: 'Dear Patrice, I have met someone else recently and…' Sorry, but the rest has faded from my memory.

Suffocating beneath a blanket of depression, there seemed no solution. I was two months in and condemned to another ten months in the army, and could see no way out. Being in the army was beyond my ability to cope. These are my somewhat hazy memories of that day when either I tried to kill myself or I made a bloody cry for help.

One day, during manoeuvres in Mourmelon, I took a razor blade with me. When it was time to shoot, I threw my gun on the floor and I started to run. I am not sure where I was running to. I held the razor blade firmly with my right hand. I placed it on the wrist of my left arm, applied pressure and slid the blade. And then blood. Next, I had collapsed, blacked out, fainted.

Was I serious about trying to kill myself? To tell you the truth, I genuinely don't know. All I knew is that I was crying. I had no girlfriend. I felt in prison. I felt there was no future. And maybe I wasn't serious. The cut was very painful, I can tell you that much. I felt terrific pain before collapsing. (Much later on, incidentally, I was in Bristol, and had some blood tests. I looked at the blood and the next thing I knew, I was on the floor. When I came round, I thought that somebody had hit me. Nobody had hit me. I just hit the floor. To do this day, I cannot bear the sight of blood and, for a blood test, look the other way.)

I came round in the surgery of the army base, and that's where I remained, under observation. During that time, I cried a lot, slept a great deal, ate nothing and frequently told the medical staff I wanted to be left alone. As I recovered, I did nothing more than play chess with the doctor, watch television and listen to music – *Abbey Road* had just come out, and would be The Beatles' penultimate album (like me, they were close to breaking point). I was so bored out of my mind that I began to consider the prospect of getting well and throwing myself into army life, trying to make a go of it.

*

I am reminded of my sessions with Anne-Marie. Before our regular get-togethers, I liked to go for breakfast at Richoux, the café which was close to her home in St John's Wood. Paul McCartney was a neighbour of Anne-Marie, and a regular at the restaurant. It got to the point of recognition, where the two of us exchanged polite good-mornings and had brief conversations.

At that time, and over a period of six to nine months, I was in the process of feverishly writing my thoughts about my life. I wrote down just about everything which came to mind. But one morning, Paul stood up, left his table and came over to mine. He said, 'You're writing a lot and thinking a lot.' He looked down at the paper. 'What is it that you're writing?'

I replied, 'All my thoughts.' Then flippantly, I added, 'I can't write songs.'

He shook hands with me. 'We all need oxygen,' he said, 'and writing is oxygen.' My notes probably included memories of my breakdown in the army, when I listened to Paul's words and music in *Abbey Road*, my Abbey Road to recovery. *Boy, you gotta carry that weight.*

Later on I read an article in the *Daily Telegraph*, in which Paul said that he had used writing as therapy when he was having a hard time with his divorce. I had not known about his divorce when I saw him in Richoux. He did not need to cross the café's floor to talk to me but, looking back, it felt like we were both mentally wounded. There was a special connection. We needed to shake hands. He felt secure enough in coming over, and in starting a conversation. He sensed I wouldn't become a stalker.

I told Anne-Marie about that encounter and asked if Paul McCartney, her neighbour, was also her client. She smiled. I saw him on several occasions and we continued our regular good-mornings, smiling politely and chatting briefly.

What about my copious notes which had aroused Paul's curiosity? I never dared re-read the madness I was writing. A few years later, I took all the pages of recollections and thoughts, and put them through a shredding machine. Nine months of labour turned to paper tatters within a few minutes. Gone, but at least I'd had the oxygen.

*

One day I looked up from my pillow, or was it the chessboard, to see the famous capitaine walking in my direction. 'Saiman,' he began, 'I gave instructions for your possessions to be removed from your cupboard and brought to the hospital.' I thought for a moment. Hmm, which cupboard? Oh, yes – the captain was talking about the cupboard beside my bed in the barracks. OK, so he had instructed the crazy hole-in-the-head sergeant to empty my cupboard. Well, my cupboard didn't contain much; simply my belongings and… Suddenly, I remembered that it also contained the letter from the medal-chested doctor at Val-de-Grâce, the letter which was addressed to the captain, who was the officer standing in front of me, and who now said, 'We found the letter that was addressed to… me.'

Yes. Schmuck here had kept that letter as a souvenir. *'My dear commandant, have you not noticed that this young soldier is…?'*

I said, 'Ah yes, sir. *That* letter. I forgot to give it to you.'

He was not in the mood for excuses. 'As soon as you get out of this hospital,' he said, 'you're going to come back to the camp. And when you come back to the camp, I'll deal with you personally.' The last words I can recall the captain saying to me: 'You'll go through hell.'

And with that, any thoughts I had about either staying in the infirmary or committing myself to the army now evaporated. Instead, I thought, *oh no, I'm not going to go back there*. I like to work with what I have available, and what I had available was the kindness and sympathy of the young doctor at the infirmary, my co-conspirator. 'I'm going to send you to a psychiatrist at Val-de-Grâce,' he said. This would buy me time.

And so I went back to that magnificent building in Paris, for a session with a couple of army psychiatrists. Then I returned for a second session of therapy, at which I thought I'd present them with a precise prognosis to save us all a lot of time. 'Look, this is very simple,' I said. 'I hate the army. I tried to commit suicide once. If you keep me here – I'll try it again, and maybe I'll succeed.'

One of the psychiatrists said, 'We know you are depressed but we don't believe you would try something so foolish again. There is no reason to discharge you.'

I said, 'You know what? I don't care whether you believe me or not. As of now, it's on the record that I'll try it again. Now, you might not think that I am going to do it. But imagine if I did.' I had their attention. 'Imagine if I did kill myself. Where are you going to be? Really, what's the point in keeping me?'

I'd given the psychiatrists not just food for thought, but a twelve-course feast of contemplation. At our third session, three psychiatrists were there and they had come round to my way of thinking. One of them began, 'I just want to say to you that before we think of getting you out of the army, you will never be able to hold a job in the French civil service.' I listened, inwardly acknowledging that we were on the road to progress. 'So you can never be a postman.' I nodded. 'Nor a minister.' Nod, nod. 'Certainly not a prime minister.' (These days this wouldn't be a problem for a prospective prime minister, I don't think.) 'Do you understand? If you are discharged you will never be able to hold a job in the French civil service. This is something you need to consider.'

I considered it for about two, or maybe three seconds, and then said, 'I understand. That's fine. I can live without being a civil servant.'

A week later, I received another letter, this one stating that I had been discharged from the army. However, I was out of the army, but not quite. They made me wait a couple of months "for the paperwork". In the meantime, I was assigned to teach English to the officers and their children. At the time it was unusual for a soldier to teach officers, and so I could not look like a soldier. Instead of a uniform, I dressed casually in jeans and so on. This period was not unpleasant, and my mental health improved. Quickly, my depression seemed to vanish.

Six months after I'd become a soldier, I left the barracks on 15th June, the same day that the murder trial against Charles Manson and his followers began in Los Angeles.

The French army was obliged to pay for my fare to return home and, as I lived in England, there was plenty of dithering from the military pen-pushers, as they tried to find cheap fares. Unable to wait any longer, I said I'd return to Paris. Done! Free at last. I came back to the flat in Swiss Cottage and, on 30th June, I was back at work, with lovely Saul and ferocious Pam. The army trauma was over. I never did try to get a job as a civil servant in France or, for that matter, anywhere else in the world.

Twenty-One

Lemmy's Boys

Being Saul's favourite would prove to be more beneficial than I could have imagined. One day Saul was asked by the owner of the group, Mr Franz Lissauer, to move temporarily to the German office. There were lots of unexplained claims, and Mr Lissauer knew that Saul was the best man to investigate.

In his absence, Saul put me in charge of credit control back in London. So I was hassling clients to cough up, which, in turn, infuriated the company's traders because the way they saw it, my pushiness threatened their own dealings with clients. 'You're screwing up our deals because you're harassing our customers.'

Their animosity didn't faze me, and even though Saul was abroad, I had his support which stretched across the continent, and, ultimately, he was the big boss. Then his wife was taken ill and so Saul had to return to London, leaving a gap in Germany. A case of ill fortune for Mrs and Mr Goodman led to my good fortune. Saul thought that I should replace him in Germany, and he got the approval of Mr Lissauer in New York. Thankfully, this new appointment came just as my twelve-month British work permit was about to expire, so I'd be saved the hassle of applying for a renewal. Even better, Roger, who was one of my flatmates, had also been offered a job in Germany, working for Ford. And not just Germany, but specifically Cologne, the same city where I'd be based. 'I'll have a company flat in a really nice suburb,' said Roger. 'We can share it. Flatmates in London, flatmates in Cologne.' The apartment was in the small town of Junkersdorf, which had a pleasant park and woodlands. As it was a company flat, Roger charged me a very reasonable rent.

And so in June 1971, a year after returning to London after military service, I arrived in Cologne. There was slaughter in Vietnam, The Doors' frontman Jim Morrison was a month away from his death (in his bathtub in Paris), and Evel Knievel, the daredevil showman, was jumping cars on his motorbike. That was a view of the world as I enrolled in a school for evening classes to learn German, and began work, starting where Saul had left off, into the investigation of alleged wrongdoings. I suppose you could say that I was picking up the scent in Cologne.

My time in Cologne would be mixed. There was the loneliness of being in a new country, trying to meet people and learn a new language. Then there was my work, which was my saviour.

Yes, there was work, and I found a routine because, after all, routine is my mechanism for coping with solitude. I learned to respect and to savour routine as a little boy in the chalet in the snowy Alpine town of Villard-de-Lans. Routine can be trusted. Every morning I'd take the tram to the office, which was in the middle of town, close to the cathedral. After work, in the evening, I'd do my food shopping, and then Roger and I would share the cooking, sometimes followed by a walk in the nearby woods. In the building where we lived there was also a table tennis table downstairs, and we'd compete regularly. My record collection consisted of precisely one album: Leonard Cohen's 1971 album, *Songs of Love and Hate*, which I played almost incessantly. I became an ardent fan of the great man and remain so to this day. Many people find his music depressing, but not me.

The job was utterly fascinating. At weekends, I'd go into the office and, being alone, I could go to the accounts department, and look for credit notes regarding one particular company that I considered to be dodgy. 'What are you doing!' yelled the head of the accounts department when he discovered I'd been snooping. 'You're not allowed to go rifling through the accounts files. Who do you think you are?' As it transpired, this young whippersnapper's rifling paid off. I was able to provide the full picture to my boss – with all the relevant claims and documents. As a result, the general manager was fired on the grounds of fraud. Once sacked, he went to work for the firm for which he'd provided regular credit notes (New York closed down their office a few months later).

I worked hard but still managed to have fun in Cologne. And after a year I had mastered German, was in a happy relationship with a German girl, and had a wide circle of friends, mostly French. Plus, I got on well with Roger. But the job was done, and therefore I was transferred to the Antwerp office, not to focus on credit control but to learn about shipping (although I returned to Cologne at weekends to stay with my girlfriend).

As the new recruit in the Antwerp office, I felt neither liked nor appreciated. The manager had been told to give me a job, but his reluctance and disinterest was clear, and he instructed me to work on business statistics, which was a meaningless chore. I lived in a boarding house and yes, was terribly bored.

So I began to write notes to Mr Lemberger, asking how I might be able to escape Antwerp and, fingers crossed, return to the office in London. He found me a two-month stint in the Amsterdam office, where I learned shipping terms and chartering, and then I was back in London.

I returned to Britain under my own steam. There was barely

any work for me in Amsterdam and I did not want to stay in order to do very little. Back in London, I stayed in my old flat in Lancaster Road (which meant we were five guys in the flat, for a bit). Then I went to the office and knocked on Mr Lemberger's door.

'What are you doing here?' he asked.

'Well, I am looking for a job.'

'You don't have a work permit, Pat,' he pointed out, correctly. 'So we can't employ you.' Oh. 'But you can come and work in my department and I'll give you some pocket money. What do you say to that?'

Lemberger had three other young guys who worked for him. They were Paul Goldenberg, Francis Presgurvic and Claude Lemberger, the son of Jean Lemberger. Collectively, we were known as "Lemmy's Boys". I'd look at all the telexes, devour each contract file and was in charge of filing. Every morning I'd take the tube from Swiss Cottage to Chancery Lane, sometimes even paying the full fare. And sometimes I'd arrive at Chancery Lane declaring to the guard, 'I've lost my ticket. But I just took the train from Holborn.' Holborn was the closest station, which mean the lowest fare. This wheeze worked until one day a London Underground inspector started asking me awkward questions. 'Where do you live? So how did you get from where you live to Holborn?' My answers didn't satisfy him, he told me off, and afterwards I limited that trick.

Lemberger arranged for the company called Leopold Lazarus to apply for my work permit which took, I think, a couple of months. It would be sent to Norma's address in Paris, so I returned to the French capital to collect it. Then I came back to London, with a proper job.

I had a new role, that involved shipping and surveying material, discharging ships and organising transport. There were plenty of strikes in that period, and one of my jobs was to deal with the headaches that arose as a result of striking workforces. Lorry drivers in the coastal town of Immingham, just north of Grimsby, went on strike, so I had to find different ways of delivering our stock. I organised lorries from Leeds, and supervised the transport. There was a confrontation, during which one of the picketing lorry drivers threatened to treat me to a swim in the harbour "with concrete boots". It was time, I reckoned, to leave the area.

During that period, I worked with a surveyor, Eric Penwill, who was well-respected in the business. He told me that a company, Lonconex, was looking for a young trader and, 'You should apply.' Eric went further. He organised a meeting with Martin Shaw, whom I met at the office, 29 Mincing Lane. It was a successful meeting and Martin said I'd have to come back to meet the managing director, Charles Davies.

Charles was a short, white-haired gentleman, who smoked a cigar, and carried himself with the authority of an ex-army officer, probably because he was proud to have served in the army. He was real old school material. 'Tell me about your background,' he said. Without a second's hesitation, I began to tell him how I had escaped the army so that I'd be able to have a career. I may have been sitting in an office in Mincing Lane, but I certainly didn't mince words as I delivered a diatribe about the army. Martin was beside me, uncomfortably shuffling his bottom on the chair, and later he said, 'I thought you'd ended your career at Lonconex before you'd even started.'

A few days after the interview, I received a letter offering me the job as a junior trader. The annual salary would be £1,850 pounds per year. At Leopold Lazarus I was earning £1,250 per year.

When I broke the news to Saul, he said he did not want to lose me and that I should meet the managing director. I also spoke to Mr Lemberger. 'Accept the offer,' was his advice. 'It's a good opportunity.' At the meeting with the managing director, Mr Walter Griessman, I said that while I had been offered the higher yearly salary of £1,850, I'd be happy to stay at Leopold Lazarus for the lower annual wage of £1,250, but that I would want to become a trader.

'Accept the job from Lonconex,' he said, or something similar. And so I left, feeling slightly anxious about what awaited me.

A few years after leaving the company, I was invited by Jean Lemberger to a cocktail party, where once again I met Mr Griessman. By then I had been made a director at Lonconex and Primary, and I was a successful trader. I reminded Mr Griessman of his quick dismissal of that young man who had ambitions to become a trader and was prepared to stay at a lower salary. His response: 'You should be grateful to me for letting you go. I understand from Jean that you have created a successful career for yourself. So you should be thankful.' Maybe I should have thanked him, but more because I learned that as a senior person you need to hold on to employees who have potential. (Admittedly I made other mistakes when choosing staff.)

Twenty-Two

The Flat

There I am, in a new job as assistant trader to a Danish guy, Pete Peterson. It is September 1973 and I am twenty-four years old. Although I was officially an assistant, I still had the word "trader" in my job title, and I worked for a major international group of companies, Primary Industries Group, which was owned by two Jewish families, Ginzberg and Golodetz, and boasted fourteen offices around the world, with head offices in New York.

It was as if my dream had come true at a young age. I could not have contemplated then that nineteen years later, and at the age of forty-two, I would lead a management buyout, and four years later that I would become the majority shareholder.

All of that was to come, however. I moved from Swiss Cottage into a new flat, though not far away, to 36, Fitzjohn's Avenue, close to the tube stations of Finchley Road and Belsize Park. The flat occupied the top floor of a converted house, and there were two bedrooms and a large living room. I took in two flatmates. Francis Dijos, like me, was a young Frenchman. Francis came from

Aix-en-Provence and had an unusual interest in fruit and vegetables. He worked in a market, selling fruit and veg, and when he landed a job at Selfridge's he'd bring home avocados and equally exotic fruits.

We got on well together, chased girls together, cooked together and then we found a new flatmate. David Polya was a Welshman, in his early twenties. He was blessed with good looks, but lacking in personality. David was a babe magnet. 'Fancy a drink at the pub?' Francis and I would ask him.

'Yeah, sure,' he'd say, and the three of us would head off. Girls swooned around him at the pub, and from time to time they came back to the flat. That's when Francis and I would step in, all smiles, personality and, above all, accentuated French accents. David had fulfilled his role. He could make the coffee and then go to bed, and Francis and I stayed up. Someone had to keep the girls company.

My finances picked up, too. Francis paid rent to me, and David paid rent to me. This relieved me, very neatly, of having to spend any of my own money on rent. So I lived for free and the landlord, Mr Zimmermann, did not mind who paid the rent. He wasn't fussed about the set-up, as long as he received his cash.

Close to our flat there was a property where students and young professionals stayed. I got to know some them and they let us use their pool and the tennis court which adjoined their accommodation. It was here that I played my first games of tennis, a sport I now play almost every week of my life.

Francis Presgurvic, my fellow Lemmy's Boy, gave me my first taste of tennis. I joined the Globe Tennis Club, in Haverstock Hill, and the other Francis, my flatmate, also began lessons. I didn't waste time in offering my services as treasurer of the club. I was treasurer for six months but relinquished the role because I'd be half-way through a match when someone would interrupt play with a tedious question about administration matters.

I stayed in touch with Jean and Claude Lemberger, and Francis

Presgurvic. One evening I went for dinner at Jean Lemberger's flat in Kensington. Paul was dating Lemberger's secretary, Margot. He said he was upset because he had discovered that Margot was also seeing "an old man". The identity of that "old man" was revealed swiftly by our host, Jean Lemberger. 'I am the old man that Margot is seeing,' he said. 'And I'll be moving in with her.' The dinner came to an abrupt end, and Paul had certainly lost his appetite.

Jean and Margot not only set up home together, they married, and they had a daughter. And they stayed together until Jean's death in 2018. Francis Presgurvic had died a year earlier.

Margot asked me to deliver a eulogy at the funeral of her husband. Jean had survived the war and the Holocaust. He had been saved by a German doctor from going to the camps. His first son had died at a young age. Jean, as I have said, was a survivor, who wanted to help young people. I know of at least four "Lemmy's Boys". Jean was also a natural-born trader, and cultivated a close friendship with Simon Goldenberg in Berlin, who was the actual agent for the Lissauer group for the whole of eastern Europe. At that time it was barter business called clearing, namely government debt trading through trading companies that bought the debts at a discount and then traded them.

Jean Lemberger was perfect in that world. He spoke German, French and Portuguese, and he travelled the world. I often told him, 'Please take me in your suitcase.'

At lunchtime I would take my sandwiches into his office and, while I ate, I'd listen to the conversations. He was a showman, too.

*

As I progressed from assistant trader to trader, the financial market was also developing at a pace. In my early days of trading, the market was booming and, like my colleagues, all that was required was buy one day, wait for a few days, and then sell at a profit.

This was easy money, although at the time I regarded myself as an incredibly gifted trader, talented at foreseeing how the market would move. For three months this streak continued, and I'd be gleefully jumping up and down the corridor as soon as I'd closed a deal. I saw myself as God's gift to trading.

Alas, I wasn't talented enough to foresee that after the Christmas break the market would collapse. Because that is precisely what happened. The buyers who had been buying in December no longer wanted to buy. More importantly, the buyers decided to cancel, or – if we were lucky – would renegotiate, leaving us with major losses. The market dived by about thirty percent. That is when my boss, Peter the great Dane, said, 'You thought you were God's gift to trading. Now it's really time to learn how to trade.' The downturn lasted more than a year and I did indeed learn how to take hits and create new opportunities for counteracting the trade. That was probably the best lesson I learnt about the dangers of trading, and it served me well in my trading career.

Twenty-Three

'Do you speak French?'

Some German clients were in town, and Pete, my boss, said to me, 'Why don't you take them out for a nice dinner? I've got to meet some Japanese clients. We could meet up, after you've seen the Germans.' I spoke their language, literally, and this was the buzzy era of "entertaining" contacts over long lunches and lazy dinners, when posh restaurants were propped up by the lavish, seemingly-limitless expense accounts of their guests. (There was, however, a good deal to be said for the business lunch as deals were so often done over drinks at the table or bar.)

Anyhow, I treated the Germans to a restaurant and then, as the evening was still young, and so on, I suggested we go for drinks at a club. We piled into my company car, a red Citroën Dyane 6, and I drove us to the Rheingold. It was a club in Sedley Place, off Oxford Street (and it was opened, incidentally, by a pair of German brothers in the 1950s but closed its doors in the late 90s).

Across the room I spotted two young ladies sitting in a corner, and I swaggered over to their table. In fractured English, I asked,

'Parlez vous Français?' That was my weak opening. But it just so happened that one of them replied, 'Un peu.'

'Je m'appelle Liz,' she added and smiled, and I was struck by her incredible eyes.

'Ah. Je m'appelle Patrice; parlez-vous français?'

'Un peu.'

We conversed in French for a bit, with Liz's friend, Sue, staring into the mid-distance, then we switched to English as the ice was broken. Liz has since told me that because I asked her if she spoke French, she presumed I did not speak much English. When we switched to English I left her wondering about this rather cocksure young man.

I discovered Liz was training as a psychiatric nurse at the Maudsley Hospital in Denmark Hill, south-east London. Well, Sue left, and then the Germans said farewell. It was now about 11pm and I had arranged to meet Pete, my boss. He had been entertaining Japanese clients in the Tower Hotel, beside Tower Bridge. 'Would you like to come with me?' I asked Liz.

'Why not?' Off we went. One day our son Oliver would become school friends with a fellow pupil whose grandfather owned the club in which Liz and I met.

We went first to the Tower Hotel and then, with Pete and the Japanese clients, to the Rififi, an upmarket club in Mayfair. Then I drove Liz home, over the Thames, to her digs at the Maudsley. We stood beside the car and said goodbye, and I asked, 'What's your phone number?' And as she told me the number, I wrote the digits with my finger on the dust at the top of the windscreen. I didn't have a pen, and – in that moment in the darkness of the early hours – that was the best I could do. In fact I would remember that number as I had (and still have) a good memory for numbers and I would not fail to remember this particular one. Liz, however, did not know that, and thought, as you might, that a splatter of rain would come along and wash away any chances of a future together.

We started going out together, Liz initially bringing her chaperone, Sue. Francis was quite happy to provide the avocados, the salad and the cheese, and we had French music with wine. I remember fondly that period of getting to know Liz. I was in a circle of friends that included lots of girls, although the relationships were platonic. This was typically French: we did not date each other, but talked about romantic relationships with others who were not in the platonic friendship circle. Liz came in and became part of the group. I am not sure if at that stage Liz fully understood that the French girls – Nathalie, Isabelle and Claudine – were just friends, but that was the case. We were all in the same group, having dinner *à La Bonne Franquette*, and playing cards, getting drunk, eating spaghetti and late-night Chinese take-aways, and all to the soundtrack of the music and songs of Brel, Brassens, Aznavour Moustaki and Adamo, as well as Françoise Hardy singing "Tous les Garçons et les Filles".

My flat was a hub for the young French community. I liked Liz being there, and she liked being there. I went to her parents' house in the countryside, and they liked me. I got on well with her father, Sandy, and mother, Betty. My friendship with her father lasted for the rest of his life. There was between us a mutual love and respect, plenty of levity, and we had long, fascinating conversations on many subjects. We clashed, too, but always with respect from both sides. My relationship with my mother-in-law was similarly very strong, loving and caring. She trusted me fully and I could be extremely cheeky with her, right until the end. She was a practising Christian who practised quietly, and did not force religion on others. I became her financial adviser and a trustee, and was privileged to have been so entrusted by the whole family (it was a role I fulfilled to the best of my ability). Yes, I had a close relationship with my mother-in-law. I loved her and I know that she loved me. I think Liz's parents saw that I was right for Liz. Forty-five years later, I am sure they were right to see things that way, and I was, too.

When you meet somebody you don't always know why you click with them. Looking back today, I would say that of all the women I have met in my life, Liz was the right choice for me. There was so much more beyond the physical attraction. For me, the mind, and the brain and the depth of character, are highly attractive. I am in agreement with Audrey Hepburn, who said, 'The true beauty of a woman is not in a facial way, but is reflected in her soul.' It was the depth of Liz's character that most attracted me.

I am much more attracted by the inside. I do wonder whether this stems from having a mother and sister who wanted to be beautiful for men.

In those early days, Liz did not know much of my childhood, and its dramas, tragedies and comedy. She believed, too, that I was a graduate of Bristol university because that is what I had told her. It was time to step away from the act. One day we were in Piccadilly Circus, in a coffee bar, when I said, 'Liz, I want to tell you the truth about me.' She looked at me, her eyes widening with terror. What crazy horrors did she think that I was about to reveal? 'I didn't really go to university.' Silence. 'And I didn't get my *baccalauréat*, either.' I think she was probably relieved.

Looking for perfection is like looking for disaster. Imperfection is desirable. So it's a question of what does one want in life, and what does one get in life? I came to the conclusion that there's no such thing as a perfect family. When you have an imperfect childhood how do you create a perfect person and create a perfect couple? It's impossible. Instead, you have to look at a scale of perfection.

Today, after almost forty-five years of marriage, one can take a breather and look at the highs and the lows, the differences between us, our joint achievements as a couple, as individuals, our own failings (I have quite a lot), our family – children, grandchildren – and can be proud of their achievements. None of us can escape our childhood. And as parents all we can do is do our best. Perhaps we can evaluate our parents' mistakes and avoid repeating some of them, while inheriting some other traits, pleasant and not so pleasant. At Ollie's wedding, Liz beautifully recited Shakespeare's sonnet:*Let me not to the marriage of true minds admit impediments. Love is not love which alters when it alteration finds, or bends with the remover to remove...*

And I think that Liz saw in me somebody foreign, outside the English circle, and she saw a lot of vitality, energy. I think she saw somebody who was maybe unattainable. I was a free spirit, a challenge. I probably still am a challenge and it is unlikely that I would have wanted a wife who would be like me. But over our married life, Liz has shown herself to be a fantastic mother, and a very supporting and loving wife, especially in pretty tense times. Therefore the phrase certainly applies: behind every successful man stands a very strong and loving wife. She enabled me to be who I am, which was not easy for her at times.

I was a different person, burdened by the hefty baggage of my childhood. If they had done proper due diligence on my background, Liz's parents may well have come to the conclusion that I was "a raw deal". Thank God for the lack of scrutiny at the time. Her parents and siblings, Richard, Wendy and Nigel, accepted me into their family.

Around this time, I felt quite proud of what I had achieved. So I wrote down a list of my assets. This list of my possessions read:

A coffee machine

A record player

Records – 33 inch (albums) and 45 inch (singles)

A silk flowery shirt

A suit

New shoes

A duvet with a yellow cover

A radio/tape recorder in the Dyane 6 (my company car).

The record player was acquired from a friend and the shoes I bought after collecting my inheritance. The duvet was free: I'd responded to an advertisement as a duvet salesman and was sent this as a sample. I kept it rather than sell it. I wrote monetary values against each item, totted them up and arrived at a grand total of £250 (that's a little over £2,000 in 2020).

My assets have grown since, and back then I had a job and a career ahead of me. I was in my mid-twenties and I was in love. This was the first time in my life there had been such a combination. I hope you will understand when I tell you that always, at the back of my mind, and considering the insecurity of the past, there was the possibility that something would go wrong. It did not.

Liz and I both wanted a family, and I think we both fell in love with each other, and that love was sealed by the prospect of creating a family together, and – more than that – a stable family. Which takes me back to my mother and sister, Norma.

*

Let's return to New Year's Day, 1968. It was then that Norma and I went to the phone box around the corner from our flat in Bristol, and telephoned our mother in Île d'Oléron. Down the line, we heard the anguish in her voice as she told us that she was suffering from sciatica. Norma, as I mentioned, returned to France, to look after Maman. When Norma tried to return to Britain, she was unable to acquire a permit because of that messy business with Michael. But something else strange happened, as was the tendency in our lives.

Norma, then aged about twenty-five, went to Paris, where she moved in with her best friend since boarding school, Chantale Devries. It was Chantale's father, Gerald, who had been a senior editor at *Paris-Soir*, the magazine which during the Occupation became a propaganda sheet, published under the instructions of the Nazis. (It was always quite difficult to get Gerald to talk about that period, perhaps because after the Liberation he would have been sent to a camp in Vichy, along with many other French intellectuals.)

Norma, at the time and understandably, required a shoulder to cry on and Chantale would have been just that; a source of comfort to my sister, whose boyfriend Michael was in prison.

But Chantale's father was also a listener, and someone who could help Norma focus on the future rather than dwell on the past and its problems. Now, my sister had always been attracted to the older man, the father figure, and Gerald – a married man, about thirty years her senior – certainly fitted into that category. Soon they began a love affair. Then the relationship became so intense and, ultimately, so real that Gerald left his wife, Nicole. He set up home with his daughter's best friend, my sister, Norma. They married and would remain together until Gerald's death decades later.

They would also buy an apartment in Dinard for holidays on the coastline of Brittany. And Norma and Chantale remained friends until Gerald's death, but that's another story.

*

Three months into my relationship with Liz, she had still not met Norma, but an opportunity arose. I had to go to Paris on business, and suggested that Liz come and join me. Norma, who was by now living with Gerald in the French capital, threw a party at which we were to be guests of honour. (Liz, I recall, came by train with my friend Francis Presgurvic. She was panicky that I wouldn't be at the station in Paris, waiting for her. Of course I was.) Later I heard that Francis asked her, 'Liz, are you in love with Patrice?'

She replied, 'Maybe.' Until then, she had not thought much about it.

This is the moment, perhaps, to look at the importance of loving and being loved. My track record with girls was poor in terms of relationship longevity. I was probably dumped by girls many more times than when I did the dumping of girls. I was frequently ditched, I think, because I was too clingy, and too serious for a few years of my life. Then I realised that being clingy and extremely serious are not particularly appealing characteristics. So I went the other way. I concentrated on my career and looked at girls differently. Getting into a serious relationship was quite scary for me. I think today I can analyse this much more objectively and I was helped to do so by Anne-Marie.

Anyhow, after Paris, Liz and I went to Deauville. We were accompanied by Norma and her beloved poodle, Naitcha, who'd been there for the fugitive adventures that ended in New York. It was in Deauville that my girlfriend would meet my mother, who was then a woman approaching her mid-fifties. We went to a pet shop in town because Norma wanted to get a collar and lead for Naitcha.

If I may just pause, because it occurs to me that about three decades earlier, during the war, my mother was in a marketplace in Deauville, not far from this pet shop, when she pocketed an apple. This petty theft was witnessed by a German commandant, and he put his hand on her shoulder... and from there, from that moment, their eyes met and a romance began. Norma and I never knew how our mother responded when the army officer said that he'd seen her steal the apple. But maybe she justified the theft like this: 'That fruit seller has hundreds of apples. He won't miss one.'

Now, in the pet shop, my mother picked up – no, not an apple – a dog collar encrusted with '"diamonds" and, hey presto, the collar vanished. While Norma had been talking to the shopkeeper, Liz and I saw my mother put the collar in her handbag. 'Come on,' she said. 'Let's go. This shop is too expensive.' Once out of the shop, she turned to her future daughter-in-law and said, 'They've got lots of dog collars and lots of money...' And then, retrieving the stolen collar from her bag, she asked incredulously, 'How dare they charge such a price for these?'

It was around about that time, the mid-70s, that my mother got a job as a cashier in Le Royal, a well-established hotel in Deauville. She held the job for about a year, and had a scam going with the head barman, and this is how it worked. He would bring his own bottles of alcohol to the bar. Then he'd serve plenty of drinks, but using his own booze. My mother would cash in the proceeds and, in return, she would take a cut from the profits. This ruse was so productive that my mother and the barman bought an old American car. The sting came to an end after a few months, namely because she and the barman were let go. A few years later, Liz and I came across my mother's partner-in-crime. It was at a five-star hotel in the ski resort of Courchevel, where we were enjoying drinks and he was pouring them.

*

Martin Shaw was the firm's deputy managing director and thought that I would be ideal at developing international business for the London office. He telexed the head trader of the group, Fred Rosenblatt, who was in the New York office. Martin suggested that I would be the right guy to chase the state-buying organisation Trading Corp of Pakistan, to open a letter of credit for a cargo of steel while the market was coming down.

The telex from NY came back: 'OK. Send Saiman. But who is he?' That was my first business trip, and I'd spend a couple of weeks in Karachi, and some time in Lahore. I managed to do a deal which was good enough for the top guys in the New York office never to have to ask again who I was.

I returned from Pakistan, Liz met me at the airport and we drove (in the Dyane 6) to Calais, crossed the Channel by ferry, and then motored down to the South of France. There we met Norma and Gerald on the island of Porquerolles, which is described as "the floating forest" but then it was also known for its nudist beaches. I mean, this was the mid-70s when naturism thrived. Porquerolles. Bees. Honeypot.

Norma and Gerald had no problem with public nudity, and after a fair amount of persuasion Liz said, 'Well, I'll take off my bikini top, but not my bikini bottom.' That was her introduction to French life. That, and the time when we arranged to play tennis with a couple who were staying in the same hotel. On the tennis court, Liz and I stood at one end and watched as the couple casually removed their swimming costumes, their nakedness on view, and then put on tennis whites.

We drove to Juan-les-Pins, which I had not seen since I was a child. Its magic had faded, vanished, and (like my mother in that pet shop) I said to Liz, 'Let's get out of here.' I did not want the new Juan-les-Pins to erase my memories of the old Juan-les-Pins. I've never been back, though I could return now, possibly. (A few years ago I went back to Île d'Oléron and it hadn't changed that much.)

During that trip, Liz was the navigator in the Dyane 6, the one who read the road map. Sat nav was years and years away from usage. Instead, I am talking about a time when every single driver possessed road atlases which were made of paper, strange though it seems. Now, the Dyane 6 was a convertible and on one occasion, as we sped southwards, a sudden gust of wind snatched the map from our car and whooshed it into the air. The map flew behind us, and a few seconds later it landed on the windscreen of the car behind us. All I can remember is the guy hooting his horn. No damage was done, but I can't recall stopping and asking for the return of the map. It may have been too much of a challenge for the French sense of humour.

Twenty-Four

The Wedding

One evening Liz and I we were in a wine bar in Beauchamp Place, Knightsbridge, when I said, 'Liz, what do you think to the idea of us getting married?' Clearly, Liz approved of the idea. Although some years later when I referred to the proposal, she said, 'Well, you never really asked.' Reflecting on it now, while on the outside I appeared to be secure, there was more than an understandable depth of insecurity in the wording of my question.

When we broke the news to Liz's parents, I added that Liz was lucky to be marrying a guy like me. I was joking, of course. Her father replied, 'Well, actually I think she's got a bit of a raw deal.' This "raw deal" phrase was new to me, and I asked Liz to explain. I hoped he was joking (which he was, of course).

We were married on 24th January, 1976. To set the scene of that time, the British music charts were topped by Queen's *Bohemian Rhapsody* and Billy Connolly's *D.I.V.O.R.C.E.* It was a month after *The Wizard of Oz* had its debut broadcast on British television, two months before Harold Wilson's resignation as prime minister (making way for James Callaghan), and it would be seven years before the arrival of the first mobile phone. Giscard d'Estaing was the French president, Gerald Ford was president of the United States, and the average price of a pint of beer was 32 pence.

Liz's parents suggested the wedding should be in the Savoy Chapel, also known as The Queen's Chapel of the Savoy, which sits behind The Savoy hotel. As the name suggests, it is the private chapel of the sovereign (The Queen has three private chapels in Britain). It is exempt from episcopal jurisdiction – it has its own set of rules. Weddings do take place at the chapel, but not by the traditional calling of banns. Instead, a special licence is granted by the Archbishop of Canterbury's office. The licence is only granted under certain conditions, and the couple needs to charm the church's chaplain before even reaching the Archbishop's office. There are application forms to be filled in, and affidavits to be sworn. As you can see, it's a Herculean challenge, but Liz's parents had been married there, I had been baptised, and we had met the Queen's chaplain, so that was that.

The church has a notable history. It stands on the site of a 14th century palace that was built by John of Gaunt, a younger son of King Edward III. It did not last long. During the Peasants' Revolt the church burned to the ground. A couple of centuries later, and under the command of Henry VII, a hospital was built on the site: the 'Hospital of Henry late King of England of the Savoy'. It was a charitable foundation made up of a complex of buildings, and its mission was to provide a night's lodging for one hundred 'pour and nedie' men. The foundation was dissolved in 1702. Much of the complex was demolished in the early 19th century for redevelopment, and to make way for the approach road to the new Waterloo Bridge. Anyhow, moving swiftly to the climax, there is one building that survives today – the Chapel of St John the Baptist, now known as The Queen's Chapel of the Savoy, or the Savoy Chapel, as Liz and I, the happy couple, knew it.

A few dozen guests attended, and after the service we enjoyed a reception at The Savoy. My mother, Norma, Gerald and his children came. As did Jean Lemberger and his wife, Margot. Jean made an impromptu speech. Ever the showman, if there was a floor to be had, Jean had it.

The honeymoon. It was to have been spent abroad. Up until a month earlier Liz had been working for British Airways overseas division, and we intended to use her allowance of airmiles. As she had since left the airline, the foreign holiday was ruled out. We left the Savoy, and merrily careered along the motorway in my brown Rover GC 2000, heading towards the West Country. Suddenly we realised that we'd left behind Liz's suitcase. So we turned around, and careered (not so merrily) back to The Savoy. At the reception desk we were no longer the top-notch VIPs we'd been a few hours earlier when they waved us off. We were now a couple of confetti-haired irritants who were holding up the smooth-running operation (I still remember their impatience, a sort of air of, 'Yes, what do you want?')

We spent our wedding night at the Grand Hotel in Bristol, and the next morning we drove to the village of Chittlehamholt in Devon. There, we stayed at a hotel called Highbullen, where they were very proud that Laurence Olivier had once been a guest. Interestingly, 1976 was to have an incredible heatwave, the hottest for 350 years. But that would be in the summer that was yet to come. When Liz and I got married five months earlier, the weather was absolutely diabolical. We almost froze in the middle of Devon in the middle of that winter. Plus, the hotel was quite grim. It was owned by a couple, but the wife was not there and the husband spent a little too much time clanking bottles and glasses at the bar. Liz and I spent a few nights at the Highbullen.

Then we made our way to Southampton, to spend a night there and specifically to eat at the restaurant opened by JC, the Frenchman who gave me a job at Le Gourmet in Bristol. After returning briefly to London, we went for a night at a hotel in Stratford-on-Avon and – *voilà* – that was the end of the honeymoon. We opened our wedding presents and began our married life at our newly bought garden flat at 5, Upper Park Road, where we'd live for three years. It was just around the corner from the home where Liz and I live today.

*

I had secured my career through the Goldenbergs. Albert gave me the entry into the trading world via his friend Jean Lemberger, who was a colleague of Simon Goldenberg. The two brothers were indebted to my father. Simon remained in East Berlin, to where he had fled to avoid facing trial for the murder of the Chilian snitch. He became a big wheeler-dealer with high connections to government circles and, in 1974, I finally met him. I stayed at his flat which was huge and very plush, extraordinary for the Soviet quarter of Berlin. Mostly, if you wanted to do business in East Berlin, you had to go through Simon Goldenberg. The two brothers remained grateful to my father for the rest of their lives, and both were instrumental to my career, while Jean made it all possible.

In absentia, Simon had been condemned to death. Under French law, provided he was not extradited (which he was not) he could only be arrested and subsequently executed if he set foot on French soil within twenty-five years of being sentenced. In 1977, more than a quarter of a century after fleeing France, Simon returned to the country for the first time. He came for the funeral of Albert. Soon after Liz came into my life, Albert had left it.

Both Albert's son Patrick, and his daughter Sylvie, asked me if I knew which brother had committed the murder. Was it Simon or Albert who pulled the trigger? Or was it the police who killed the denouncer, Roi? 'I don't know,' I said to Patrick and Sylvie. 'All I can tell you is that your father was so gentle that he couldn't kill a fly. However, Simon, by all accounts, was charming but dodgy. But you know what, whether it was Simon or your father who killed that bastard, I probably would have killed that bastard. He decimated the family? Albert's first wife was separated from their daughter Sylvie, and sent to the camps, and to her death. Sylvie, as I have previously mentioned, has a scar on her cheek, a constant reminder of the moment – she was five years old – when a German soldier viciously slashed her with a knife.

My father and Albert had a friendship that flourished in the original Goldenberg restaurant in rue des Rosiers. Neither man was around, of course, to know of the horror that unfolded in that restaurant at lunchtime on 9th August 1982. It was the scene of a bloody attack by Palestinian terrorists, who threw a grenade into the restaurant and then entered and opened fire with machine guns. Six people were killed, a further twenty-two were wounded. The perpetrators have never been put on trial. The restaurant closed its doors in 2006. (The restaurant was sold by Albert in 1969 to Jo, his younger brother.)

Albert and my father, so close during life, are both buried in the old Jewish cemetery in Bagneux, just south of Paris. Simon, who saw his brother buried, is now alongside him. The remains of the three men who were so crucial in the shaping of my life are within one hundred yards of each other. Jean Lemberger, another of the central characters in my life, is buried in Lyon.

Twenty-Five

⌒◡⌒

Au Revoir

My mother would say, '*Les gens bien portants sont des malades qui s'ignorent.*' People in good health are sick people who ignore their sickness. When her oncologist told her that she had to lose weight, she replied, 'Some people are fat and can lose weight. Some people are bald and they can't grow hair.' The oncologist was bald.

When she was seventy-something she drove down what she believed was a one-way street. It was indeed a one-way street, just not the way she was going. This resulted in a head-on collision with a motorbike. The motorcyclist was catapulted above my mother's car, and soon afterwards he was being rushed by ambulance to hospital. My mother was distraught. She realised the extent of her mistake, and the damage to the poor guy, who was bleeding from his waist and below. It turned out that his reproductive organs, as my mother said, had been irrevocably damaged in the accident.

'I want to go and see him in hospital, and take a bouquet of flowers,' she said. 'I want to apologise.' Norma and I dissuaded her because we had an image of a young man lying in his hospital bed, and being confronted by the elderly woman whose incompetence had prevented him from becoming a father. He might have thought, 'Is she here to finish me off?' She did not visit.

Long before my mother's own decline into poor health – way before Alzheimer's took its grip – the subject of her funeral had come up one day when Norma and I were with her. 'I want to have a simple funeral,' she said.

Our mother did not really do simple, and Norma and I asked, 'What do you call simple?'

'Well,' she responded, 'Patrice, I want your father's remains to be exhumed.' This was not an easy ask. 'And I want my body and his remains to be cremated. And I want our ashes to be buried in Deauville.'

I looked her straight in those dark brown eyes. '*Maman*,' I said, '*pas de problème*.'

Obviously, the thought of requesting an exhumation in a Jewish cemetery was preposterous. Afterwards Norma said to me, 'What are you saying? Why are you telling her that?'

'It's not going to happen, Norma. But I'm not going to argue about it.'

It's difficult to evaluate when the real dementia came in, and when my mother left. On one occasion, I told her that I was coming over to Paris, to see her and to have dinner with her. Why? Because, more than anything else, I felt dutybound to do so. I arrived at her apartment building and rang the buzzer. There was no response. I rang again and again, but still nothing. So I phoned. No reply. And then I left. Back at my hotel, I called again. This time the phone was answered. She said, 'Where are you?'

'In Paris, Maman. We are due to have dinner. I came over and rang on the buzzer. But no one was answering the door.'

She said, 'Oh, come back.'

And I said, 'No. That's it.' At that point was she completely forgetful? I am not sure, but then the doctor said that she would need to be cared for in a home. So I took her into a home, and then I sold her apartment in Paris.

Towards the end, I sat at my mother's bedside and held her hand. I said, 'You are fed up with the whole thing, aren't you?'

She said, 'Yes.'

I left my mother's bedside and asked the senior nurse what she thought about my mother's deteriorating health. The nurse replied that they would try to alleviate the pain. 'Your mother could last for a few days,' said the nurse. 'Or for a few weeks.' My mother died three days later. She was fed up and she'd had enough.

I felt an overwhelming sense of freedom. The children said to me, 'Are you all right, Daddy?'

I replied, 'I hate to tell you, but the truth is that I am free at last.' The weight, the guilt – they had disappeared. It is unfortunate, but Marcelle Boissière was never destined to be a mother. She was destined to be a mistress. She was destined to be with a man, destined to be looked after. Maybe when she sent Norma and me away, she really knew that she could not look after us. Perhaps the only way that she could actually look after us, was not to look after us.

Anne-Marie asked me, 'What was your happiest time with your mother?' Many years after being asked the question, I still don't have the answer. When I think of her, anxiety comes to mind. That, and needing to care for her. I looked after her, financially. So I would agree with my mother, that children are very useful. I was an object which served her purpose. Did she love me? Probably. Most likely. In her own way. Could she actually love? She loved Maurice. And when Maurice was there, as I have said, she was happy which made me happy. And she had a good sense of humour. But what was my happiest time with my mother? I wish I could find the answer. I would love to be able to say, 'You know, we had such happy times, and let me tell you about them…' But I don't have the answer.

When our mother died, Norma and I agreed that her funeral would take place at the Jewish cemetery. Norma organised the coffin, chose the casket in which our mother would depart. I visited the funeral parlour and the undertaker asked, 'Would you like to see your mother for a last time?'

I was led into a room, and there, in the casket was my mother. She looked restful. I felt no emotions whatsoever. Once I had seen her, the undertaker lifted the coffin lid and placed it on top of the coffin. That's when I saw it. There, emblazoned on the lid, was a carving of Jesus Christ on the cross. The Messiah He may have been, but not in the eyes of the Jews. And so afterwards I said to Norma, 'Well, that's a brilliant start – we're going to a Jewish cemetery with Jesus on the cross.'

Norma said, 'Oh no, I didn't notice.'

Now, all these years later, it still sticks in my mind. At the time, of course, I found myself saying to Norma, 'Don't worry. It doesn't matter. Forget about it. Let's just put some flowers on top of the coffin, and no one will see Jesus.'

It was when Norma and I were in the hearse – beside us, my mother in a coffin festooned with flowers – that I suddenly thought, *Shit. There are no flowers in a Jewish cemetery.* Flowers are often forbidden. Strange though it seems, I spent the journey to my mother's burial hoping that hers would be the only burial in the cemetery. Then there would be no other mourners to be offended by the forbidden flowers that covered up the seemingly offensive carving of Jesus Christ. I was thinking, 'I hope we can whizz in and out before anyone sees us.' As we entered the cemetery, I got a glimpse through the windscreen ahead of us. 'Shit,' I said. 'Look Norma, there's another funeral.'

We drove towards a mass of mourners – and Jewish funerals tend to be extremely well-populated – and I said to the driver, 'Just hoot gently, please.' I was anxious to part the crowd, so that we could move quickly to our spot. The driver just touched the horn, and the mourners shuffled slowly and made a pathway for our car, like aged sheep moving for the sheepdog. They could see the hearse, and I was convinced that at any moment we would be asked about Jesus and the flowers in a Jewish cemetery.

The hearse came to a halt and the funeral director took the coffin out of the hearse. He asked us if we wanted a few minutes to pay our last respects. Out of the corner of my eye, I saw a couple of rabbis walking towards us. In Jewish cemeteries there are rabbis who walk about and, when they spot a funeral, they approach the grave to ask if you'd like them to say a prayer. So I told the director to speed up a little with the coffin, and then I gently wandered towards the rabbis: 'Thank you for your kind offer of prayers, but...' I blocked their way, ensuring they did not get any closer to the coffin as they may well have questioned the presence of Jesus. I smiled at them, and said, 'We're fine, thank you... *Très bien, merci.*'

Earlier on, I had delivered a eulogy at the church. It was a short, off-the-cuff speech. I cannot recall exactly what I said to the assembled mourners – not a large crowd – but it went like this: 'Something must have happened to our mother which prevented her from being the mother we might have liked to have had. She had a full, eventful life. She had a good sense of humour. And she was a very good cook.

'And while we were eating whatever she had cooked – which was always excellent, by the way – there was no question that we had to express our admiration... express our admiration for the whole meal, and listen to the explanation of how long it took our mother to make, and precisely how our mother made it.

'She was blunt and direct. She had a sharp tongue and she would fire missiles. Yes, she would fire missiles, not thinking where they might land, or how they might affect others. And those *others* included her own children. She was extremely generous. She was a passionate woman, and she was more a man's woman than a mother. She was a survivor, no question about it. She had no knowledge of any boundaries… whatsoever.'

My mother's name is not on the gravestone. Why? Well, I suppose that says everything, doesn't it? However, she did not receive her final wishes of being cremated with my father's remains. She was buried, however, alongside him in the same plot. So in a way, her wish of a reunion was granted. Being the wife and the widow of my father gave her a great sense of fulfilment. 'Je suis Madame Saiman,' she'd say with pride, right up to those final days.

If my attitude seems callous, it is worth remembering my mother's profoundly acidic wit and lack of empathy. This applied to the death of loved ones, as well. Norma's husband Gerald had a brother called Yvan, and when he died his body had to be kept in a mortuary freezer for eight days before the cremation took place in Dinard. '*On peut l'appeler une omelette norvégienne,*' said my mother. We can call him a baked Alaska. Hot on the outside, frozen on the inside.

So there in Paris, Norma and I laid our mother to rest. A grave adorned with flowers in a place where flowers were forbidden. She was, after all, the great rule breaker, the rebel. And now I am reminded of the time I bought carnations for my mother. We were living at the time in Avenue des Gobelins, and I was nine or ten years old. My mother took the bouquet, and then she threw it in the bin. 'I don't like carnations,' she said, 'they remind me of funerals.'

*

I had begun analysis with Anne-Marie in January and was seeing her three or four times a week. As the summer approached, she told me that she would be going on holiday. 'OK. That's not a problem,' I said. 'Enjoy your holiday and we'll see each other when you get back.'

Liz and I went around the same time to the South of France, staying in a beautiful hotel, Le Club de Cavalière, on a fantastic beach beside the Mediterranean. The hotel is near Le Lavandou, which is where Norma and I, as children, spent a whole August with our mother in a hilltop villa. Norma and I built sandcastles and swam, and we plucked plump grapes from the vines in the vineyards, and our mother cooked supper which we ate, a family of three, on the terrace that looked out to sea.

Here I was, decades later, and Liz and I were staying in this luxurious hotel. But I kept crying. Not just a little sob here and there, but full-on emotional outbursts of hysterical tears. I spoke to Anne-Marie on the phone a few times and that helped a bit.

When we regrouped in September, the teary phone calls were the first topic of discussion. The thing is, neither of us had realised how difficult our "separation" would be for me. Anybody who has not been in analysis, would say, 'That's ridiculous. It's stupid. You're a grown man, a success, a husband, a responsible father.' But it was not stupid to me. I felt completely abandoned, and so there you have it – that's just the way it was. Anne-Marie said, 'You were feeling abandoned by me. I had not realised this would happen and I am sorry you had to go through it.'

We talked about the level of abandonment that I'd had as a child. Or that I felt I'd had. After being "abandoned" by my father, due to his death, I was then "abandoned" by my mother when she sent me to the chalet on the slopes. She never came to visit and I don't recall receiving a single letter from her. And then Anne-Marie, who had become my surrogate mother, had gone on a long holiday! So yes, I did feel abandoned, ridiculous though it may sound. That was how I felt, but now I can see it differently. Our mother never truly abandoned us. She was a presence through our lives. In this way, she showed us love.

When I met Anne-Marie, her intention was that I have a few sessions, after which she'd find the ideal therapist for me. I continued to see her frequently for the next fifteen years. And then there came a point when she said something like, 'I'm probably going to retire. I'm starting to feel a little old.' Anne-Marie was about ninety years old. She said to me sweetly, 'We can always meet, if ever you fancy it.' She left door to her cosy room open to me.

Time passed and then, at the end of July, 2018, I wrote an email to Anne-Marie. 'I haven't seen you for a while, but would you happen to have time for a session?' I got an email back, but not from Anne-Marie. It was from her personal assistant. 'Very sadly, Anne-Marie died three days ago…'

I did not cry at my mother's death, but I cried when I heard about Anne-Marie's death. Years earlier, when Liz and I were in the South of France, I had cried when I felt abandoned by Anne-Marie. Now I was in the South of France once again, and learning of her death.

Susie Orbach wrote an obituary of Anne-Marie in the *Guardian*, describing her as 'the clinician's clinician'. The tribute began, 'Technically adept and unafraid of the difficult states of mind and feelings psychoanalysis can uncover, she influenced several generations of practitioners, returning them to the interest in minds, hearts and longings that had led them to train in the first place. Her passion was how people worked. Her curiosity, her genuine interest in the other person, the excitement of seeing an individual come to life after suffering, was infectious. It helped move many a trainee and experienced analyst away from the reductionism, constraining theory and cold analysis that had gripped some training institutes…'

I wrote to Anne-Marie's assistant, something along the lines of, 'I really don't want to intrude in any way, but please would you mind checking with the family if it would be all right for me to attend the funeral?' She sent me the funeral details, and added, 'Anne-Marie would have loved you to have been there.'

'I am going to fly back for the funeral,' I said to Liz, who immediately offered to come with me, and to support me. I told her no, that I needed to be alone to pay my respects to Anne-Marie, just as I had been alone in my therapy with her. The funeral took place at a crematorium on a Sunday. I did not know another soul who was there for the farewell, and that did not matter. After the service I was standing on my own outside the crematorium. Maybe I was feeling invisible. Then a lady came up to me. She said, 'Oh you must be Patrice.'

'Yes, yes. I am.'

'I'm Anne-Marie's daughter, Catherine.'

'I am very, very sorry about your mother, about her death,' I said, and I could feel tears well up. I didn't have any right to cry when Catherine was the one who had lost her mother.

She said, 'I'm so happy you came. Our mother would have been delighted that you came. She would have loved that you are here.'

It's most likely that I was Anne-Marie's final patient. We built a special relationship, a unique bond. We had a strange relationship which was real and, at the same time, it was almost unreal because of the professional association. Later on, I wrote an email to her personal assistant: 'If there is a stone setting or something like this, please let me know.' I never got a reply. I don't know whether she had left, or... I didn't want to intrude.

Epilogue

In the spring of 2018 I began to write notes. I like to write notes, and these particular ones were about my childhood and years as a young man. Eventually, these scribbled recollections and thoughts would become the story that you have now read.

Anne-Marie Sandler, my analyst (as you know), believed it would be a fascinating story. 'You should write it,' she would say. She also said it would be a productive, therapeutic follow-up of the fifteen years of work that we had done together.

In addition, I was encouraged by my family and friends to write the story (secretly, they may have been asking me to stop talking about it). At the same time, I was driven by the wish to understand what really happened during my youth, and to make sense of it. To dig up the roots, give them a proper shake and a good inspection. As it transpired, the entire process would become a connection to the people who were no longer in my life.

Sometimes it felt easier to write this as a story of that little boy, almost as if it were an out-of-body experience. I tried to convey the feelings of the boy, and then the teenager and young man who was in the midst of adults he had to rely on. Those adults who had managed to survive the war were also coping with their own lives and preoccupations.

We will never know what this was like and hopefully we will never experience this first-hand. As an adult, and like many other people, I share the frustration that human beings continue along the same path of fighting.

Often, we are led down the path by politicians determined to go to battle. The effect outside millions of deaths and devastation is a creation of refugee camps where young generations will grow. What is to become of these little children as adults?

I think this is a useful reminder which puts me in my place.

Now, back to me and that little boy. The events related in the first twenty-two years of his life were probably more than many people would have experienced in a lifetime.

Whilst there were the ripple effects of the Second World War that little boy witnessed anti-Semitism, adultery, divorce, treason, kidnap, deaths, murder, fraud, prison, deceit, abandonment, loneliness, bankruptcy, coupled with adventures, travels, exciting times, and fun (which could be precarious and sometimes dangerous).

Those years of uncertainties prepared him to deal with life.

It could be argued that this was a crash course in life and could have ended badly. As luck had it, the crash course paid off in many ways but only the future could tell.

One could also suggest that a more conventional and stable upbringing would leave a young adult less prepared to face the world, and rather exposed without any experience.

How would each child fare in future life?

Incidentally, it would be useful to go through the childhood of many world leaders, dead or alive (I won't mention the names, especially of the politicians who are still in power) and we could use the old adage: blame the parents.

The responsible adults (for that child) in that story had forgotten him, and had many other issues to deal with. They had their own past and their own abilities to deal with life. They did what they could.

Luckily, the child survived but learned quickly, strived as a child and as a young adult, listened and absorbed events, and he had the ability to think what was right and wrong, what made sense. He was given the nickname '*Pépère*' (Granddad) from his mother when he sensibly suggested everyone had drunk enough and needed to go to bed, as he had to get up early to get to school.

Human instinct prevailed. I looked up the Oxford Dictionary definition of instinct. 'An inborn impulse or motivation to action typically performed in response to specific external stimuli. Today instinct is generally described as a stereotyped, apparently unlearned, genetically determined behaviour pattern.'

His father and mother had survived in their own ways the war. They had mettle (strength). The various characters in his life such as Albert, Simon, Sylvie, Norma, Patricia, Danièle, Léon Stain… they all survived life in their own ways.

Help and support came from unexpected people.

Renée and Joseph who, after all, were chauffeur and cook/cleaner but became part of the family. Joseph had fought the Germans during the First World War with Renée's brother, who suffered from mental illness for the rest of his life and ended up in a mental institution in Berck.

Albert and Simon, out of loyalty to my father, were the catalyst in the start of my career.

Jean Lemberger provided all the help I needed to get my first job when in fact I probably was the least qualified person in Britain for that job.

Saul Goodman and Pam Powell trained me and provided me with the training necessary for the international trade.

Martin Shaw who, back in 1973, helped me acquire a job in trading back. He believed in me and allowed me to progress up the ladder.

All this help enabled me to travel the world, connect with

many cultures, whether in Asia, the Middle East, China, Eastern and Western Europe, North and South America, or north Africa. What an absolutely fascinating world! Twenty years later the owners of the group acknowledged, 'We don't know how we blew $250 million in ten years.'

And I simply asked, 'What about me leading a management buyout?' I had no idea what I was talking about at the time but I learned.

(Indirect help came from my witnessing the failure of others: my mother's bankruptcy; the Ginsbergs, who inherited so much and lost it all; later on other major financial collapses from a wealthy family I got to know very well.)

A year later, and as I turned forty-three years old, I succeeded in leading a management buyout with the support of major financial institutions and twelve international banks, in a total package of £73 million, and with fourteen offices around the world, 140 staff and a turnover of $1.5 billion.

That was another new adventure. I am working on the second book already. I was thrown into international trade which I see as a bit like Outer Space. It brought dangers, opportunities, excitement. It offered exploration, of people, countries and cultures. I had embarked on a mission to understand what was now new to me. Thank God for my childhood.

*

Monsieur Perrier, our English teacher, made us study the poem "If", by Rudyard Kipling. He explained to a class of thirteen-year-olds, 'This is a letter from a father to his son of how to be a man.' Well, you can imagine how much I loved that poem, and how much I have referred to it and still refer to it and recommend it. It is applicable to so many circumstances, and establishes the key to leading a satisfactory life, remain balanced, deal with the ups and downs in life with undisturbed minds, while also having the confidence and patience to handle any situation.

A moral lesson from a father to a son on how to grow up to be a better person, and a true man. Kipling reminds his son that he will be a man if he can hold on to his values and not be swayed by others, and, if he follows his advice, he will have a rewarding and enriching life. He must be able to stand by his convictions, holding on to his virtue and his humility in the process. He must not let the opinions of others hold too much sway. He must live his life fully, making the most of the opportunities and days he is given on Earth. And if can do all these, then, my son, he will be a man.

Imagine how influential this poem was to me, a teenager who had lost his father and who was searching for advice. This poem became a mantra for me as a teenager, and it influenced the rest of my life.

On a lighter note, it reminds me of the management buyout. One of the owners wrote a book, and on the collapse of their business quoted Kipling's poem, but changed it slightly: 'If you can keep your head when all about you are losing theirs, then you probably have lost the plot.' They certainly had, but it was too late.

It was a valuable lesson for me. To this day I have never lost the plot, nor did I ever lose the memories of what it felt like to be poor. However, I understand that money is not a god and there are many other values much more important, such as loyalty, being true to oneself and the love of family.

Much of this book was written during the coronavirus pandemic. During this period many have spoken of the necessity to make positives out of one massive, world-wide negative, and to identify, recognise and appreciate what we have, rather than dwell on what we have lost. Perhaps that approach has helped me through life.

Looking at it another way, there may well be a baluster or two that are missing along the staircase, but you mustn't let that stop you climbing the steps.

Acknowledgements

A memoir focuses on the life of one person. But the making of the book (just like a life, of course) requires the help of many in order to go smoothly. Fortunately, there is space for me to thank those who have assisted in the creation of this particular story, and others who have played a vital role in my existence.

I shall begin with Liz. Over the last forty-seven years, she has shown me immense love and care, not to mention patience. She has complete understanding of the (sometimes complex) man she married. In times of trouble, she has always been there for me. Liz, I am eternally grateful to you, and I love you.

For many years, our children Nathalie, Sophie and Oliver encouraged me to write about my early days. They inspired me to reflect and write, and then they gave constructive criticism. This memoir has added purpose to my life, and I am deeply indebted to the three of you. I am also pleased that you were able to laugh at the stories, and sorry if there were some that made you cry.

Anne-Marie Sandler was the analyst who became the mother I did not think I had, and she provided me with greater insight into my birth mother. My mother never actually abandoned me and in her own ways she loved both my sister, Norma, and me.

I am delighted to be able to thank Norma, who provided me with additional elements of our childhood which I had forgotten. My sister, Patricia, helped me to recount elements of her life. My sister, Danièle, gave me the military documents and told me stories about my father. My cousins in France also shared many stories of my father.

I am extremely grateful to Fatima Kaddouri and Neelam Patel for deciphering my handwritten notes, and transforming them into typed-up, legible documents. And I am pleased to have the opportunity to thank several kind and trusted friends who read the manuscript and then provided me with the reassurance to have it published. They are Philippa Cardale, Praxoulla Charalambous, Arthur Crocker, Malcolm Glover and Graham Haynes and my old friend Denis Cohen.

Dr Simon Gibeon, my GP, got me into hospital, and Neil Kitchen took it from there. I owe my life to both men. There are not enough words to express my gratitude.

Renée and Joseph were always there for me as a child. They understood me and protected me, and had also protected Danièle. They are long gone, but there is never a day when I do not think of them. There are others who are always in my thoughts: Albert and Simon Goldenberg who were the catalyst for my future career; Jean Lemberger who was the instrument for making it happen; Martin Shaw who believed in me and helped me through my career.

The writer, James Steen, was introduced to me by Liz, and we worked together as co-authors. He made the story amusing – even for me – and he made me feel emotional, too. We spent hours and hours discussing the content, and he showed great sensitivity and understanding.

Valerie Jeancard qui habite aujourd'hui au 2 square la bruyère a permis d'obtenir les photos de l'escalier de service et est le catalyste pour potentiellement me permettre de rentrer dans l'appartement de mon pere soixante-cinq ans apres.

Bethany Askew the author provided invaluable assistance in finding my way around the publishing world.

My thanks are due to many others, such as the concierge of the cinema who provided me with food and shelter, and my schoolteacher Monsieur Perrier, who introduced me to English, and to the poem, "If", which has been such a significant "tool" in my life.

Sincerely, I say merci beaucoup to you, dear reader, for taking an interest in my story.

This memoir would not have been possible without my father and my mother. I hope this book will make them both proud. More importantly, I hope my life will make them proud. I am sure it will. I know it will. So, to both of you, thank you for my life.